MW01137857

USA TODAY'S DEBATE: VOICES AND PERSPECTIVES

HUMAN TRAVEL
TO THE
MOON AND MARS

Waste of Money or Next Frontier?

Matt Doeden

Twenty-First Century Books · Minneapolis

USA TODAY®, its logo, and associated graphics are federally registered trademarks. All rights are reserved. All USA TODAY text, graphic, and photographs are used pursuant to a license and may not be reproduced, distributed, or otherwise used without the express written consent of Gannett Co., Inc.

USA TODAY Snapshots®, graphics, and excerpts from USA TODAY articles quoted on back cover and on pages 13, 14–15, 29, 34–35, 39, 42, 42–43, 57, 58–59, 69, 76–77, 88–89 ©copyright 2012 by USA TODAY.

Twenty-First Century Books
A division of Lerner Publishing Group, Inc.
241 First Avenue North
Minneapolis, MN 55401 U.S.A.

Website address: www.lernerbooks.com

Library of Congress Cataloging-in-Publication Data

Doeden, Matt.
     Human travel to the moon and Mars: waste of money or next frontier? / by Matt Doeden.
          p.   cm. — (USA TODAY's debate: voices and perspectives)
     Includes bibliographical references and index.
     ISBN 978-0-7613-6436-8 (lib. bdg. : alk. paper)
     1. Outer space—Exploration—United States. 2. Astronautics and state—United States. I. Title.
     TL789.8.U5D64 2012
     629.45'4—dc22   2010035644

Manufactured in the United States of America
1 – MG – 7/15/11

CONTENTS

INTRODUCTION

One Giant Leap

O N JULY 20, 1969, PEOPLE AROUND THE WORLD GATH-
ered in front of their television sets. They were riveted
by what they saw. A grainy black-and-white video feed
showed the cold, barren surface of the Moon. Cameras
then showed a small landing craft undock from a larger spacecraft and descend toward the Moon's surface.
The landing craft carried two U.S. astronauts.

Unpiloted spacecraft had landed on the Moon
before, but this was the first time people had landed.
Less than a decade before, U.S. politicians had committed themselves to putting an American on the Moon.
That was about to happen.

The U.S. program to send astronauts to the Moon
was called Apollo. To prepare, earlier in the 1960s, the
U.S. National Aeronautics and Space Administration
(NASA) had sent a series of unpiloted spacecraft to
either orbit (travel around) or land on the Moon. In
late 1968, a spacecraft called *Apollo 8* carried the first
astronauts into orbit around the Moon.

Apollo 11 was the breakthrough flight. This was the
craft that carried the astronauts to the Moon on July 20,
1969. The mission had launched from Kennedy Space

Left: Neil Armstrong took this picture of Buzz Aldrin on July 20, 1969.
The two men were the first people to set foot on the Moon. You can see
Armstrong and the *Apollo 11* landing craft reflected in Aldrin's visor.

Center near Cape Canaveral, Florida, four days earlier. *Apollo 11* traveled almost 250,000 miles (402,000 kilometers) to reach the Moon. The spacecraft then orbited 69 miles (111 km) above the Moon's surface.

The landing craft, called the *Eagle*, undocked from *Apollo 11* and carried astronauts Neil Armstrong and Buzz Aldrin toward the surface. A third crew member, Michael Collins, remained aboard *Apollo 11*, which continued to orbit the Moon. The *Eagle* headed to its planned landing spot in a flat area on the Moon called the Sea of Tranquility.

The mission faced a problem, however. The landing spot was covered with small rocks. The *Eagle* couldn't touch down there. Armstrong piloted the craft above the Moon's surface. Fuel was running low. If the *Eagle* took too much time in landing, it wouldn't have enough fuel to return to *Apollo 11*. Finally, with just thirty seconds of fuel to spare, Armstrong found a flat spot. The *Eagle* kicked up dust as it landed on the Moon's surface. Over the radio, Armstrong announced, "The *Eagle* has landed."

A camera was fixed to the outside of the lander to capture the historic moment. Millions of television viewers watched Armstrong emerge from the lander and slowly climb down a small ladder. Finally, his booted foot touched down on the Moon's surface. As he left the first human footprint on another world,

Above: Neil Armstrong takes a "giant leap for mankind" as he steps out of the *Apollo 11* lander onto the Moon's surface in 1969.

Armstrong spoke into his radio, saying, "That's one small step for man, one giant leap for mankind."

They had done it! Aldrin followed Armstrong out of the lander, becoming the second person to set foot on the Moon. The two astronauts spent the next two and a half hours on the Moon's surface. The Moon's gravity—a force that pulls things toward the ground—is low, so when the men walked, they nearly bounced. They took scientific readings and placed a U.S. flag on the Moon's surface. Finally, they got back in the *Eagle*, blasted back into space, docked back with *Apollo 11*, and traveled home to Earth.

The mission was a success. The U.S. space program had done something that a decade before seemed almost impossible. Many people believed that the Moon landing was the dawn of a new era. They thought that travel to and from the Moon—and in time Mars— would become commonplace. They believed that humanity was destined to explore and settle the solar system and the stars.

The truth, however, proved to be quite different. Five more Moon landings followed, with the last coming in December 1972. Then the Apollo program ended. Human beings have not stepped foot on another world since. Many people, from scientists to politicians, believe it's time for that to change.

CHAPTER ONE

Stay or Go?

WHY HAVEN'T PEOPLE BEEN BACK TO THE MOON since the early 1970s? Technology since then has grown by leaps and bounds, yet astronauts have only orbited Earth during that time. Probes, or unpiloted spacecraft, have studied the surfaces of the Moon, Mars, and the other planets and their natural satellites (moons), but no human astronauts have ventured more than a few hundred miles from Earth's surface since the last Apollo flight.

Few doubt that the United States, either alone or with international cooperation, could send crewed missions to either Mars or the Moon. The debate is over whether we should do so. For many, the answer is a resounding yes. Proponents of crewed space travel point to potential scientific discoveries, the potential for space industry, and possibly even the creation of space colonies for human settlement. Many argue that human beings are explorers by nature and that if we can visit other worlds, we must.

Some people even argue that exploring and settling new worlds is critical to the survival of the

Left: Humans have not visited the Moon since the early 1970s. Should we go back to the Moon and travel even farther into space?

> **"We do not know where this journey will end, yet we know this—human beings are headed into the cosmos [space]. Mankind is drawn to the heavens for the same reason we were once drawn into unknown lands and across the open sea. We choose to explore space because doing so improves our lives and lifts our national spirit."**
>
> **—U.S. PRESIDENT GEORGE W. BUSH,** 2004

human species. They say that Earth is running out of the resources needed to support human life. They worry that war, disease, or another crisis could wipe out humanity. Legendary physicist Stephen Hawking explained this viewpoint in 2010. "It will be difficult enough to avoid disaster [to the planet or to human civilization] in the next hundred years, let alone the next thousand or million," Hawking said. "Our only chance of long-term survival is not to remain inward-looking on planet Earth, but to spread out into space. We have made remarkable progress in the last hundred years, but if we want to continue beyond the next hundred years, our future is in space. That is why I'm in favor of manned, or should I say, 'personed' spaceflight."

Others see things differently. The arguments against further space travel generally boil down to two main points: money and safety. Space travel is expensive. Any mission would require a massive upfront financial investment, with no guarantee of a return on that investment. With so many problems to solve on Earth, spending a lot of money on space exploration seems unthinkable, opponents say. Also, space travel is as dangerous as it is expensive. Spacecraft are built from thousands of parts, and the failure of even one can spell disaster. Even in a spacecraft that works flawlessly, astronauts would still be exposed to brutal and potentially deadly conditions, both in space and on the surface of Mars or the Moon. Scientists still don't know much about the long-term effects of extended space travel on the human body. Some argue that given such uncertainty, human life is too precious to risk.

WHERE TO GO

Even among those who support crewed missions to other worlds, not everyone agrees about where to go. The solar system is filled with planets and moons. But of these worlds, few are suitable for humans. The inner planets, Mercury and Venus, are roasted by the heat of the Sun. The distant planets are made mostly of gases. They could never support human life. Their moons are too distant from the Sun and therefore too cold to be realistic targets. That leaves us with two worlds suitable for human exploration: the Moon and Mars. Each comes with its own unique challenges and potential rewards.

THE MOON

The Moon is Earth's constant companion and closest neighbor. It is an appealing target for exploration for several reasons. First, it's much closer to Earth

> **The Apollo program was such a success because it did have complete [public] support. This may be very difficult to achieve in the near future.**
>
> **—AARON COHEN,**
> RETIRED TOP OFFICIAL WITH THE APOLLO PROGRAM, 2009

Above: This illustration shows what a Moon base might look like. We might be able to use the Moon as a power-generating station or as a base for exploring other parts of the solar system.

than any other body in the solar system. In its orbit around Earth, its average distance from our planet is just 238,855 miles (384,400 km). In cosmic terms, it's right next door. Furthermore, we know that people can travel to the Moon. The Apollo missions proved that. Finally, the Moon could be an invaluable resource to Earth. Scientists and engineers have dreamed of turning the Moon into an orbiting power plant for Earth. Some envision burning the Moon's abundant hydrogen and helium gas to create nuclear energy (powerful energy released by changes in the nucleuses, or cores, of atoms). Others propose setting up thousands of solar power collectors on the Moon. The equipment would convert the Sun's energy into electricity for use on Earth. In these ways, the Moon could play a big part in solving Earth's energy crisis. Furthermore, the Moon could be a great jumping-off point for further space voyages—to Mars and beyond.

People also make arguments against heading to the

USA TODAY Snapshots®

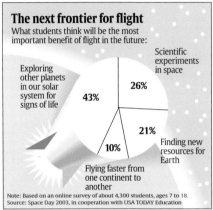

The next frontier for flight
What students think will be the most important benefit of flight in the future:

- Exploring other planets in our solar system for signs of life **43%**
- Scientific experiments in space **26%**
- Finding new resources for Earth **21%**
- Flying faster from one continent to another **10%**

Note: Based on an online survey of about 4,300 students, ages 7 to 18.
Source: Space Day 2003, in cooperation with USA TODAY Education

By April Umminger and Sam Ward, USA TODAY, 2003

Moon, however. One of the biggest is that we've already been there. Astronauts have walked on and studied the Moon's surface. They've brought a lot of rocks and dust back with them to study on Earth. The Moon probably doesn't hold many new surprises. With no atmosphere (layer of gases around its surface) and no liquid water, the Moon is a dead world. Scientific discovery and long-term human habitation, or settlement, of the Moon is unlikely.

MARS

Mars, often called the Red Planet because of its rusty red color, is the fourth planet from the Sun

(Earth is the third). It rests on the outer fringes of what scientists call the Sun's habitable zone. This is the area around a star where liquid water can exist on the surface of a planet. If a planet is too close to its star, any water will boil away. If a planet is too far away, water will freeze. Life as we know it cannot exist without liquid water, so a planet must be in the habitable zone to support life. Most scientists agree that Mars is the only planet in the solar system other than Earth that has the potential to support life.

Mars, named for the Roman god of war, has fascinated sky watchers since the dawn of civilization. People have long imagined intelligent Martian lifeforms, wars between Earth and Mars, and even human colonies on the Red Planet. Humans have sent probes into orbit around the planet and landed robot explorers on its surface. The planet has offered tantalizing hints of life— from impressions in Martian rocks that resemble tiny lifeforms to evidence that water once flowed over the planet's surface.

What's Our Next Step?

From the Pages of
USA TODAY

Forty years ago Monday, Neil Armstrong made his "giant leap for mankind." Since that triumphant moment, astronauts in the U.S. space program have gone no further.

The first footsteps on the moon—made by Armstrong on July 20, 1969, on the mission known as *Apollo 11*—came 3½ years before the last ones. Since then, astronauts have been stuck close to the Earth, mostly circling a few hundred miles overhead in a spacecraft that's little more than a glorified cargo truck.

So now what?

That question preoccupies NASA and worries the Obama administration. The president said in March that NASA is beset by "a sense of drift." Even some of the men who once walked on the moon are divided on how to proceed. Options could include going back to the moon, landing on an asteroid, shooting for Mars or even ending human exploration of space altogether.

Polls regularly show that Americans have a warm feeling for the human spaceflight program and don't want it to end. That means figuring out what astronauts should do next. Should they forge outward into the solar system, despite the huge cost and a soaring deficit? And if so, where?

Some possible destinations for human space explorers include:

The Moon

Yes, America has been there. That doesn't mean it's not worth going back, say scientists and an astronaut who's been to the lunar surface. Humans went to the moon six times from 1969 to 1972, spending fewer than 13 days there. Lunar advocates say that's hardly time enough to plumb the moon's mysteries.

NASA's plans for the moon include not just short, Apollo-style stopovers but eventually a moon base. The agency hopes to send the astronauts back to the moon around 2020.

Operating a moon base would allow astronauts to practice living on another planet, NASA's Jeff Hanley says. Crews would need that experience before pressing on to Mars, the long-term goal of most space enthusiasts.

"The fastest way to get to Mars is through the moon," says Harrison Schmitt, who in 1972 was one of the last two men on the moon. "We need to learn how to work in deep space again. That's what the moon does for us."

An Asteroid

It may sound crazy, but preliminary NASA studies indicate it's possible to send humans to visit asteroids, huge chunks of rock and gravel that orbit the Sun.

Asteroids, unlike the moon, have negligible [little] gravity, so a space-ship could fly to an asteroid and just pull up next to it. Then an astronaut could clamber out and explore. Going to the moon requires not just a space-ship but an expensive lander, one equipped with rockets so it can blast off from the lunar surface. Asteroids also are of interest because they're loaded with minerals that could be useful for space crews headed into the solar system.

Mars

Scientists have debated the existence of life on Mars for more than a century. Mars boosters say it's time to settle the arguments by sending humans to the Red Planet.

"As celestial [outer-space] bodies go, the moon is not a particularly interesting place, but Mars is," *Apollo 11* astronaut Michael Collins said in a statement from NASA.

A Mars trip may seem far-fetched, but such a mission was proposed by the first President Bush in 1989. The idea went nowhere then, but the younger President Bush's 2004 plan for NASA also included the goal of sending humans to Mars.

Nowhere

Even some strong supporters of space exploration say the best place to send America's astronauts would be nowhere at all.

Opponents of human spaceflight say robots can do the job just as well as astronauts, pose no safety worries and work cheaply. Sending humans into space isn't worth it, they say.

"The cost and risks are just too high," says physicist Robert Park of the University of Maryland, who wants NASA's manned program to be phased out.

"Manned space travel adds far more cost than is justified in terms of scientific return," says Rep. Barney Frank, D-Mass. Frank says he doesn't want to end the astronaut program but doesn't want to send humans to Mars or the moon. He'd restrict astronauts to tasks robots can't handle.

—Traci Watson

For these reasons, among others, Mars is an appealing subject of study and exploration. It has water ice beneath its surface and at its north and south poles. Its atmosphere has very little oxygen, which people need to breathe. But some scientists believe that humans could change Mars's atmosphere—a process called terraforming—to increase the level of oxygen.

But unlike the Moon, Mars is not right next door. Even when it is nearest to Earth in its orbit, it's 38 million miles (61 million km) away. At its farthest point, it is 249 million miles (400 million km) away. The trip from Earth to Mars would take about 250 days, or eight months, and the journey would be fraught with danger. For these reasons, a mission to Mars would be vastly more expensive than a mission to the Moon.

MANY QUESTIONS

The debate over whether to send human crews to Mars or the Moon is complex. We must consider many issues. Can it be done safely? How much will it cost, who should pay for it, and will it be worth the money? Should governments be involved? And if we do decide to go, what should the goals of the missions be? Should astronauts search for ways to create industry, mines, or settlements on the Moon or Mars, or should the missions be purely scientific?

Above: Humans have never been to Mars. Many people think it's time we visited the Red Planet.

Asteroid Dreams

Some scientists suggest visiting asteroids rather than the Moon or Mars. Asteroids are small rocky objects that orbit the Sun. Most of them orbit in a zone called the asteroid belt, which lies beyond the orbit of Mars. Asteroids are a promising target for several reasons. First, they have little gravity to disrupt the motion of a spacecraft. So they would be easier to land on and take off from than moons and planets. Second, asteroids could hold a wealth of scientific data. Scientists believe asteroids have changed little since the formation of the solar system, so studying them could give us insight into the origins of the solar system. Finally, most scientists agree that asteroids are probably rich in minerals, such as metal ores. One day we might be able to mine asteroids for this wealth.

Above: An asteroid streaks through the sky.

Finally, should humans even be the ones to go? When Neil Armstrong became the first person to walk on the Moon in 1969, robotics and computer technology were in their infancy. In the twenty-first century, robots and other machines are capable of doing many of the exploration tasks that people once had to do. Machines can explore other worlds without any risk to human life and at a fraction of the cost of sending human astronauts. Has the time for crewed space missions passed us by? Should robots be our eyes and ears in space? Or is it our destiny to explore and settle new worlds, spreading humanity across the solar system and, one day, to the stars?

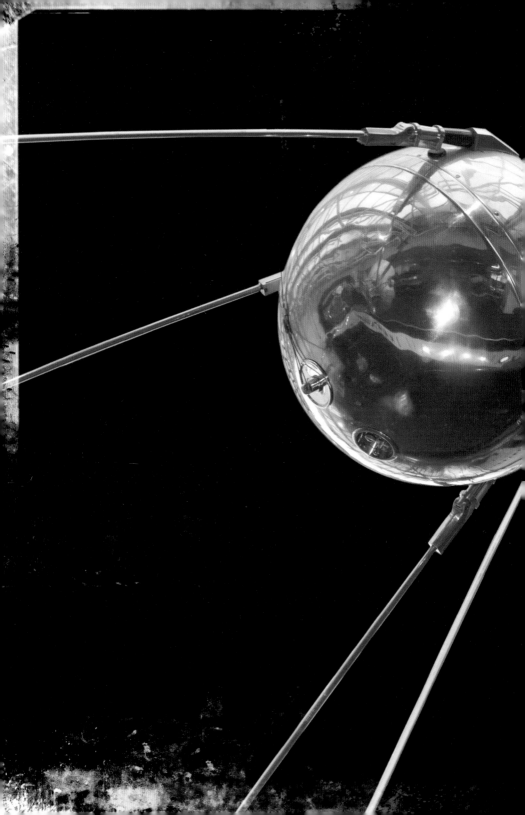

CHAPTER TWO

Blastoff: The History of Space Exploration

SINCE PREHISTORIC TIMES, PEOPLE HAVE WONDERED about the Sun and other stars, the planets, and the Moon. Over the generations, people have imagined what these bodies look like up close, what treasures they hold, and whether they are home to otherworldly people or beings. In the 1600s, with the invention of the telescope, scientists began to learn more about objects in the sky. But the history of actual human space travel and exploration is quite short. It wasn't until 1949 that humans were able to send machines into space.

In many ways, human beings have a war to thank for pushing them into space. During World War II (1939–1945), Germany, the Soviet Union (comprised of present-day Russia and fourteen other republics), the United States, and other nations scrambled to develop new weapons technologies. Military engineers designed high-powered rockets and fast, sleek

Left: The first vehicle to orbit Earth was *Sputnik*, launched by the Soviet Union in 1957. Americans were shocked that the Soviets were the first to reach this important space milestone.

jet airplanes. The United States built the first nuclear bomb during World War II. The war was bloody and painful for millions of people, but it also spurred a growth of technology unlike anything the world had ever seen.

The war ended in 1945, but the new technologies remained. What's more, an uneasy relationship between the United States and the Soviet Union began to form. The two nations had been allies during the war but grew distrustful of each other when the fighting was over. It was the beginning of a long period called the Cold War (1945–1991). During the Cold War, the United States and the Soviet Union did not fight directly with armies and weapons. But they did battle in other ways. One of these battles became known as the space race. It was an unspoken contest for superiority in space.

The United States struck first. The U.S. Army had captured V-2 rockets built by Germany during the war. The German military had used the V-2 as a long-range weapon, but the United States had another idea. Instead of loading the rocket with explosives as the Germans had done, the U.S. Army attached a second rocket, called a WAC Corporal, to the V-2. The goal was to shoot the rockets into outer space.

The army launched the first such two-stage rocket on February 24, 1949. The V-2 soared to an altitude of 20 miles (32 km) above Earth. At that point, the WAC Corporal detached from the V-2 and fired its own engine. It reached an altitude of 244 miles (393 km), becoming the first human-made object to reach outer space.

The Soviet Union made the next major breakthrough in the space race. On October 4, 1957, the Soviets launched a spacecraft called *Sputnik 1*. Rockets carried the vehicle into space and put it into orbit around Earth.

U.S. leaders immediately started a program to put their own vehicle into space. The United States built *Explorer 1*, which went into orbit on January 31, 1958. That same year, the United States created NASA and charged it with the task of putting an American into space.

THE FIRST PERSON IN SPACE

The Soviets had the same idea and beat the Americans to the punch. On April 12, 1961, Soviet cosmonaut (astronaut) Yuri Gagarin climbed aboard a tiny capsule called *Vostok 1* and prepared to blast off into space. In all human history, no person had ever left the planet we call home.

Gagarin appeared confident before the launch. He said, "In a few minutes a mighty spaceship will take me into the far-away expanses of the universe.... Can you think of a task more difficult than the one assigned to me? It is not a responsibility to a single person, or dozens of people.... It is a responsibility to all Soviet people, to all mankind, to its present and its future.... See you soon!"

The launch was a success. *Vostok 1* climbed more than 200 miles (322 km) above Earth's surface, carrying Gagarin into space. *Vostok 1* orbited Earth one time, making the trip in just under two hours.

Above: The Soviets launched *Vostok 1* from the Baikonur Cosmodrome in modern-day Kazakhstan on April 12, 1961. Aboard the rocket was Yuri Gagarin, the first human to travel into space.

Returning to Earth was somewhat more problematic. Soviet engineers hadn't yet figured out how to safely land a spacecraft. So after *Vostok 1* reentered Earth's atmosphere, Gagarin ejected himself from the craft and floated to the ground with a parachute. *Vostok 1* continued its descent without him and slammed into the ground. Both Gagarin and the craft landed near a Russian farm. Wearing his space suit and dragging his parachute behind him, Gagarin then asked the

After reentering Earth's atmosphere, the remains of *Vostok 1 (above)* landed in a field in the Russian countryside. Yuri Gagarin used a parachute to escape from the craft.

farmers if he could use a telephone to call Soviet authorities. (This wasn't the story the Soviet Union told the press, however. Keeping their inability to land a spacecraft a secret, the Soviets told the world that Gagarin had landed the craft. Only later was the truth of his return revealed.)

Gagarin's successful mission was a cause for celebration around the Soviet Union and the world. Even the United States issued formal congratulations. Although the United States successfully put its own astronaut, Alan Shepard, into space a few weeks later, many in the U.S. space program saw the Soviet launch as a bitter defeat for the United States.

RAISING THE STAKES

The space race was heating up, and U.S. president John F. Kennedy was ready to grab the biggest headline of all. On May 25, 1961, Kennedy spoke before the U.S. Congress. "I believe that this nation should commit itself to achieving the goal, before this decade is out, of landing a man on the Moon

> **We choose to go to the Moon in this decade and do the other things, not because they are easy, but because they are hard, because the goal will serve to organize and measure the best of our energies and skills, because that challenge is one we are willing to accept, one we are unwilling to postpone, and one which we intend to win.**
>
> **—U.S. PRESIDENT JOHN F. KENNEDY,** 1962

and returning him safely to the Earth," Kennedy said. "No single space project in this period will be more impressive to mankind, or more important for the long-range exploration of space; and none will be so difficult or expensive to accomplish.... In a very real sense, it will not be one man going to the Moon ... it will be an entire nation. For all of us must work to put him there."

Kennedy outlined an ambitious goal: to develop and build space technologies that did not yet exist and to put them into practice, in under nine years. It

was a bold idea that captured the imagination of millions. To many Americans, it seemed a matter of national pride to beat the Soviets to the Moon. And so the stage was set for a new era of space exploration.

PROBES GO FIRST

NASA soon caught up with and surpassed the Soviets. It sent more astronauts into orbit and sent probes to other planets. The probes carried cameras, sensors, and radios that sent information back to scientists on Earth. NASA launched *Mariner 2* in 1962. This probe swept past Venus. Its cameras and other instruments revealed that the planet was blanketed in a hot, churning atmosphere. *Mariner 3* and *Mariner 4* launched in 1964. Both probes were destined for Mars. *Mariner 3* suffered a malfunction en route and was left without any power. But *Mariner 4* made it to Mars and sent back the first real data on the Red Planet. This data showed Mars to be a cold, dead world.

Above: The *Mariner 2* space probe was designed to gather information about the planet Venus. The probe flew by Venus four months after its August 1962 launch.

"THE *EAGLE* HAS LANDED"

The Apollo program—the mission to send astronauts to the Moon—got off to a rough start. The program's first spacecraft, *Apollo 1*, was scheduled to launch in 1967. But disaster struck during a prelaunch test. The crew was inside the spacecraft when a fire broke out. The exact cause of the fire was never determined, but it spread quickly. All three astronauts aboard—Virgil "Gus" Grissom, Edward H. White, and Roger Chaffee—were killed.

Despite this tragedy, NASA continued to launch Apollo flights, putting astronauts closer and closer to the goal of landing on the Moon. Finally, on July 20, 1969, President Kennedy's goal became reality when Neil Armstrong and Buzz Aldrin became the first humans to set foot on the Moon.

More Moon missions soon followed.

Above: Apollo 15, launched in 1971, made the fourth Moon landing. One of the astronauts poses here near the landing craft, an American flag, and a lunar rover.

Apollo 12 successfully reached the Moon in November 1969. In April 1970, *Apollo 13* launched. During the outbound trip, one of the spacecraft's oxygen tanks exploded. The craft had to swing around the Moon without touching down and return to Earth. The mission was a near disaster. Returning to Earth, the spacecraft grew dangerously low on air and power. No one knew if the craft's heat shield (panels that protect a craft from heat generated during reentry into Earth's atmosphere) had been damaged in the explosion. Without a working heat shield, the spacecraft would have burned up during reentry. Across the United States, people nervously watched news broadcasts as the spacecraft and its three astronauts made their return. Somehow, despite all the problems, *Apollo 13* managed to safely return to Earth. The mission never reached the Moon, but disaster was averted. NASA dubbed the mission a "successful failure."

Four more missions successfully landed on the Moon. Astronauts brought back about 842 pounds (382 kilograms) of Moon rocks and dust. Scientists studied the materials to learn about the Moon's composition. The last Apollo mission was

Apollo 17, in December 1972. After that, the U.S. government canceled the program because of its high cost. *Apollo 17* remains the last piloted spacecraft to leave Earth's orbit.

MORE PROBES

NASA's mission changed after the Apollo program. The organization no longer worked to send astronauts to other worlds. Instead, NASA focused on sending probes into space. Probes were far cheaper and safer to launch than crewed space missions.

Pioneer 10 launched in 1972. This probe traveled through the asteroid belt, passed Jupiter, and then headed to the edge of the solar system. (*Pioneer 10* continued to send information back to Earth until 2003, when radio contact was lost.)

The Viking program returned to Mars. *Viking 1* and *Viking 2*, which launched in 1975, photographed Mars in detail from orbit. *Viking 1* sent a lander to

Above: This image shows a *Viking* lander on the rocky red soil of Mars in 1976. Both *Viking 1* and *Viking 2* orbited the planet and sent landers to the surface.

Mars on July 20. When the lander touched down, it became the first human-made object to land on another planet. The lander sent back information about the planet's atmosphere and soil. It also sent back the first color image of the surface of Mars.

The *Voyager* probes headed even farther out into the solar system. *Voyager 1* and *Voyager 2* launched in 1977. Their mission was to study Jupiter and Saturn. They sent back volumes of data about these gas giants (giant gas planets) before continuing on to the outer solar system.

SPACE STATIONS AND SPACE SHUTTLES

Also in the 1970s, while probes were heading toward the planets, both the United States and the Soviet Union started building space stations. Space stations are orbiting scientific laboratories. NASA and other space agencies use them to conduct experiments in space. Astronauts can live on space stations for months at a time. Small space stations are fully built on Earth and launched into orbit by rockets. Large stations are built on Earth in a series of sections. Spacecraft carry the individual sections into space, where astronauts assemble them.

The Soviet Union was the first nation to launch a space station. That station, Salyut 1, went into orbit on April 19, 1971. It was the first of a series of Salyut stations launched by the Soviets. The Soviet program was plagued with problems, however. One spacecraft couldn't properly dock at the station. The next spacecraft docked successfully, and its crew of three cosmonauts lived at the station for twenty-three days. However, a malfunction in their spacecraft on the return voyage killed all three.

Meanwhile, the United States had its own space station program. The first U.S. station, Skylab, launched on May 14, 1973. The station was badly damaged during launch, and a crew had to rush up to fix the problems. Two more crews followed. Altogether, the three crews spent a total of 171 days aboard the station. The last two crews mainly performed scientific experiments and took photographs of Earth and the Sun. More missions were planned for Skylab, but in July 1979, the station unexpectedly fell from its orbit. It reentered the atmosphere, and heat generated by the reentry burned up the station.

Space shuttles are reusable aircraft. They blast off using rockets. But because they have wings, they land like airplanes. NASA uses shuttles to carry artificial satellites (such as weather and communications satellites) into space, to transport astronauts to space stations, and for scientific missions. Shuttles are not designed to leave Earth orbit. NASA launched its first space shuttle, *Columbia*, in 1981. Over three decades, five U.S. space shuttles have made more than 130 launches. The shuttle program's overall success has been marred by two disastrous failures, however. The shuttle *Challenger* exploded on liftoff on January 28, 1986. *Columbia* broke apart as it reentered Earth's atmosphere on February 1, 2003. Both disasters killed all the astronauts on board.

Above: The space shuttle *Columbia* launches from Kennedy Space Center in Florida in 1997. *Columbia* flew twenty-eight successful missions. But in 2003, it broke apart during reentry. The disaster killed all seven astronauts on the shuttle.

Women in Space

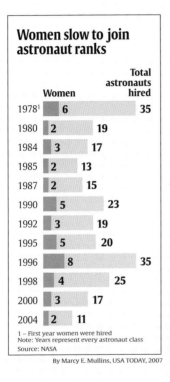

Women slow to join astronaut ranks

	Women	Total astronauts hired
1978[1]	6	35
1980	2	19
1984	3	17
1985	2	13
1987	2	15
1990	5	23
1992	3	19
1995	5	20
1996	8	35
1998	4	25
2000	3	17
2004	2	11

1 – First year women were hired
Note: Years represent every astronaut class
Source: NASA

By Marcy E. Mullins, USA TODAY, 2007

Valentina Tereshkova of the Soviet Union became the first woman in space in 1963. She orbited Earth forty-eight times in *Vostok 6*. The United States, meanwhile, didn't accept women into the astronaut program until 1978. The first U.S. woman in space was Sally Ride *(below)*, who flew on the space shuttle *Challenger* in 1983.

INTERNATIONAL COOPERATION

In 1986 the Soviet Union began construction on a large space station called Mir. Five years later, in 1991, the Soviet Union dissolved. Russia, the largest of the former Soviet states, took over Mir. With the fall of the Soviet Union, the space race was effectively over. Instead of competing, the United States and the former Soviet Union began to cooperate on space missions. As part of this new spirit of cooperation, in 1992 two Russian cosmonauts joined a U.S. space shuttle, while one U.S. astronaut served aboard Mir.

Meanwhile, NASA was planning a new space station. The organization invited four non-U.S. space agencies into a partnership. These were the agencies of Japan, Canada, and Brazil, as well as the European Space Agency (ESA), which represents eighteen European countries. Together these agencies planned to build and operate the International Space Station (ISS). After the 1992 astronaut-cosmonaut exchange between Russia and the United States, Russia's space program also joined the effort.

The ISS represented a big change for space policy. International cooperation helped divide the costs of the program among many different nations. Many believed the ISS would also help foster a sense of harmony between the contributing nations. That seemed to be the case. Russia and the United States, which had been bitter rivals for decades, were suddenly working toward a common goal.

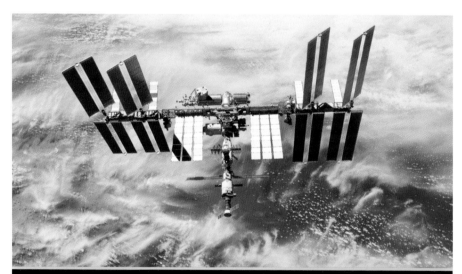

Above: The International Space Station (ISS) orbits Earth. A crew member on the space shuttle *Discovery* took this photograph of the ISS in 2010.

ALH84001 and Life on Mars

The possibility of life on Mars was headline news in the summer of 1996. That's when several NASA scientists, led by David McKay, published an article in *Science* magazine announcing that they had discovered evidence of life on Mars.

The scientists' evidence was a meteorite—a chunk of rock from space—that had been found in the ice of Antarctica. Scientists believed the meteorite, called ALH84001 *(right)*, had been blasted off the surface of Mars by an asteroid impact millions of years ago. The rock contained some interesting shapes. They looked like the fossils, or impres-

sions, of tiny living organisms. In addition, the meteorite contained chemicals that could have been produced by living things. The scientists believed that the meteorite, tucked safely in the ice, had not been tainted by Earth-based life.

Many scientists agreed that the meteorite made a strong case for Martian life. Others questioned the announcement. There was no proof the shapes in the meteorite were fossilized life-forms, they argued. And the chemicals found in the meteorite could have been formed by other processes, not necessarily by living things. Some scientists called the announcement irresponsible. Others accused NASA of trying to stir up public excitement over life on Mars in hopes of getting increased funding from the U.S. government.

> **" I'll believe in people settling Mars at about the same time I see people settling the Gobi Desert [in Asia]. The Gobi Desert is about a thousand times as hospitable as Mars and five hundred times cheaper and easier to reach. . . . There's no good reason to go there and live. It's ugly, it's inhospitable and there's no way to make it pay. Mars is just the same, really. We just romanticize it because it's so hard to reach. "**

—**BRUCE STERLING,**
SCIENCE FICTION WRITER, 2007

Construction on the ISS began in 1998 and continued, both on Earth and in space, for more than twelve years. Its first crew—a team of three—launched in October 2000. Both U.S. space shuttles and Russian spacecraft ferried crews and their supplies up and down from orbit. The typical ISS crew consists of three astronauts, but the station can support up to seven people for short periods. Typically crews stay at the station for three to seven months before being relieved. Like Skylab, the ISS's main purpose is scientific research. By 2010 the station was fully assembled.

BACK TO MARS AND THE MOON

In the 1990s and early 2000s, NASA once again turned its attention to Mars. It sent a series of probes and landers to the Red Planet. While many of these missions failed, due to launch problems, loss of radio contact, and other setbacks, some succeeded. In 1996

Above: The *Phoenix* lander went to Mars in 2008 to search for signs of life. It didn't find evidence of life, but it did collect data about water on Mars and about the Martian atmosphere.

NASA's Pathfinder program sent a rover (a wheeled, movable robot) called *Sojourner* to the Martian surface to carry out experiments and search for evidence of Martian life. The rover performed experiments and sent data for three months before radio contact with Earth was lost. In 2004 NASA landed two rovers—*Spirit* and *Opportunity*—on the Martian surface. Another lander, *Phoenix* arrived on Mars in 2008 to search for life, although it didn't find any.

Probes continued to study the Moon as well. In 2009 the United States launched the Lunar Crater Observation and Sensing Satellite (LCROSS). This spacecraft orbited the Moon but did not land there. Instead, it launched a rocket into a crater on the Moon, creating a spray of debris. Using cameras and sensors, LCROSS then analyzed the debris, looking for evidence of water ice from the crater. The mission was a success. LCROSS confirmed that the crater contains water ice.

Today, the Wheels on the Rover Will Go Round and Round on Mars

From the Pages of USA TODAY

A small roll for a rover, a big leap for mankind will take place early today—if all goes as planned—when NASA's *Spirit* rover rolls onto the sands of Mars.

A day after President Bush called for human explorers to visit Mars in coming decades, and barring unforeseen delays, *Spirit* was scheduled to roll 10 feet [3 meters] forward. If the rollout succeeds, the mobile geology lab will begin two days of analyzing its surroundings.

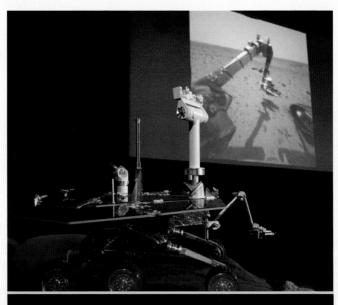

Above: This model, on display at NASA's Jet Propulsion Laboratory in California, looks like the real *Spirit* rover that went to Mars in 2004. The screen in the background shows actual images sent to Earth from *Spirit*.

After that, a slow-paced, "six-wheelin'" exploration jaunt ensues for 80 days. *Spirit* will first head for a crater 800 feet [244 m] away and then toward intriguing hills to the east.

The commands to turn the rover toward an unblocked exit ramp Tuesday night went "perfectly," says *Spirit* mission manager Jennifer Trosper of [NASA's] Jet Propulsion Laboratory in Pasadena, Calif.

After the rollout, the lander that carried *Spirit* 303 million miles [488 million kilometers] to Mars will be left behind and should be visible on navigation cameras on the rear of the rover.

Spirit's main goal is to investigate the history of water on Mars as revealed by its geology. The rover's first chance to "see things up close and personal," says mission scientist Raymond Arvidson of Washington University in St. Louis [Missouri], comes as its arm picks up samples from the surface.

The arm holds a microscopic camera, a pair of German spectrometers that will measure the chemical makeup of rocks and soils, and a grinding tool to expose the inside of the rocks.

Accurate measurement of atmospheric conditions, dust, gases and temperatures during the flyovers will allow scientists to "strip away the atmosphere" and draw more precise conclusions about the surface, Arvidson says.

"We are very excited about where we are today. . . . We're ready to explore Mars," says lab engineer Kevin Burke. He ended his remarks at the briefing by showing an image of the sun setting on Mars—as seen by *Spirit*.

—Dan Vergano

CHAPTER THREE

Big Bucks: Paying for Space Exploration

IN 1989 PRESIDENT GEORGE H. W. BUSH TRIED TO benefit from excitement surrounding the twentieth anniversary of the first Moon landing by proposing a piloted expedition to Mars. Budgeters estimated the price tag for the mission would be between $450 billion and $500 billion. With the space race all but over at that point, no one in the U.S. government was willing to spend that kind of money. The idea went nowhere.

In 2004 President George W. Bush followed in his father's footsteps by proposing a plan of his own. Bush called for an end to the space shuttle program. He proposed that the money allocated to that program, along with additional funds, be directed toward the development of a new vehicle capable of carrying astronauts to other worlds. His plan called for a crewed trip to the Moon sometime between 2015 and 2020. "With the experience and knowledge gained on the Moon, we

Left: In 2004 President George W. Bush spoke at NASA headquarters in Washington, D.C. He said that NASA needed to develop new vehicles to carry astronauts to the Moon and Mars.

will then be ready to take the next steps of space exploration—human missions to Mars and to worlds beyond," Bush said.

Just as his father's had, the younger Bush's plan faced severe opposition. Its cost was also estimated at up to $500 billion. Bush's full plan failed to get the support it needed, although NASA did take up a few aspects of the plan, such as the development of new rocket technology.

When U.S. president Barack Obama took office in 2009, many wondered what his administration might mean for NASA. Would the new president support new space programs? At first supporters of space exploration had reason for optimism—Obama had said many times that he was fascinated by outer space. But the new president faced many problems. The U.S. and world economies were mired in a terrible recession in 2009. The U.S. Congress spent vast amounts of money bailing out major banks and other businesses,

> **" Improvements in launch vehicles will make departure from Earth easy and inexpensive. Once we have a foothold in space, the mass of the asteroid belt will be at our disposal, permitting us to provide the material needs of a million times as many people as Earth can hold. . . . We have the resources to colonize the entire Milky Way [galaxy]. "**
>
> **—JOHN LEWIS,**
> U.S. ASTRONOMER, 1996

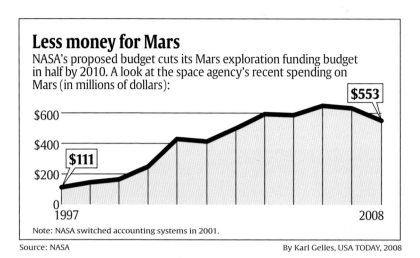

Less money for Mars

NASA's proposed budget cuts its Mars exploration funding budget in half by 2010. A look at the space agency's recent spending on Mars (in millions of dollars):

Note: NASA switched accounting systems in 2001.

Source: NASA

By Karl Gelles, USA TODAY, 2008

with the fear that failing to do so could result in a total economic collapse. With all those pressing concerns, the United States had little money left for space exploration.

A year later, in 2010, the Obama administration put forth its budget for NASA and its plans for future U.S. space exploration. Obama increased NASA's overall funding. At the same time, his administration cut NASA's Constellation program, a series of new spacecraft designed to replace the aging space shuttles. Obama said he wanted to change NASA's focus. He outlined a plan in which the U.S. government would pay private companies to handle orbital flights—work previously undertaken by space shuttles. The hope was that private companies could do the work more cheaply than NASA and would also inject a new spirit of innovation—or creative thinking—into the effort. At the same time, the Obama plan called for NASA to develop new technologies to allow for crewed deep space missions—sending astronauts to the Moon, Mars, and beyond.

"Early in the next decade, a set of crewed flights will test and prove the systems required for exploration beyond low Earth orbit," Obama said. "And by 2025, we expect new spacecraft designed for long journeys to allow us to begin the first-ever crewed missions beyond the Moon into deep space. We'll start by sending astronauts to an asteroid for the first time in history. By the mid-2030s, I believe we can send humans to orbit Mars and return them safely to Earth. And a landing on Mars will follow. And I expect to be around to see it."

Like John F. Kennedy and both president Bushes before him, Obama talked big about crewed space exploration. But what would the costs be? Would the future United States—or any other nation—be able to afford to send astronauts back to the Moon or to Mars?

A QUESTION OF CASH

The biggest obstacle in sending missions to the Moon or Mars isn't technical. Technology has made huge advances since the Apollo program sent astronauts to the Moon in 1969. Modern scientists and engineers have all the know-how they need to send astronauts back to the Moon, and to Mars for the first time.

The problem is money. Space exploration isn't cheap. Estimates place the cost of a crewed Moon mission at $100 billion. A crewed Mars mission could cost five times that much. Space exploration was no cheaper when John F. Kennedy announced his plan to send astronauts to the Moon. In 2011 dollars, the Apollo mission cost more than $170 billion. But in the 1960s, the United States and the Soviet Union were entrenched in the Cold War. Getting ahead in the space race was for many a matter of national pride. And the U.S. economy was robust during the 1960s—so the nation could afford the expenditure. For many Americans, the price tag for the space program was almost an afterthought.

The modern U.S. political and economic climate is much different from what it was during Kennedy's time. Spending hundreds of billions of dollars on space exploration is harder to justify. Many argue that the money would be better spent improving education, paying off the national debt, or researching renewable energy sources. In a time with many social and economic problems, spending huge amounts of money on space exploration seems wasteful to some.

Others believe that space exploration will open new technologies. The money spent on space exploration doesn't just go up in smoke, they argue. It creates jobs and pays the salaries of those who develop and build the technology. It pays to buy materials, many of which come from U.S. producers, which in turn creates more jobs. Funding a crewed mission to the Moon or to Mars would stimulate the economy, some contend, much in the same way military spending does.

COST CUTTING

Some say we could lower the cost of crewed space travel greatly by using existing technology rather than spending money developing new spacecraft. For instance, we could use the same type of rockets that powered the Apollo missions rather than developing new kinds of rockets. We could use habitat (housing) technology developed for the International Space Station to house crews on a Moon or Mars mission. By using existing technology, we'd be able to slash spending on research and development. But this approach has serious downsides. For instance, old technology might not perform as well as newer, more expensive technology. In addition, using old technology wouldn't spark a new wave of innovation. It could stunt the long-term growth of the space program.

Alternatively, we might be able to save money with new technologies. For instance, nuclear-powered rockets could drastically shorten travel time to the Moon or Mars and lighten the required fuel load. Or we might be able to propel spacecraft with solar, or Sun, power. These money-saving technologies would probably work, but developing them would require vast sums of money—perhaps canceling out the savings.

A Space Race to Change the World

From the Pages of
USA TODAY

More than eight years ago, a new space race began with the announcement of the X Prize Competition. Based on prizes that inspired the development of aviation in the early 20th century, the X Prize was started to encourage private space travel through a competition to build the first reusable spacecraft.

The competition will reward $10 million to the first team to privately finance, build and launch a spacecraft that can carry three people 62 miles [100 km] above the Earth's surface, return them safely to Earth, and then do it again within two weeks. More than 20 teams around the world have joined the competition.

On Wednesday, Burt Rutan's high-tech aerospace firm, Scaled Composites, took a first step toward the prize with its *SpaceShipOne* vehicle. His team launched a man into a suborbital [less than a full orbit] test flight in June.

This new space race has not been as well publicized as the one to the moon waged between the United States and the Soviet Union. Nevertheless, this race may have just as great an impact on the course of human history. The era of private space travel—of the common person as space voyager—may well be at hand.

The entry this week of Richard Branson, the owner of Virgin Airlines, is another clear momentum builder. He has plans for a suborbital tourist operation, called Virgin Galactic, that will use technology

SpaceShipOne's successful flight

69.6 miles

SpaceShipOne

3 7:52 a.m. SpaceShipOne reaches its maximum altitude, 367,000 feet. Pilot was weightless for four minutes.

2 7:48 a.m. SpaceShipOne undocks from White Knight and fires its rocket, roughly 46,000 feet.

Flight path

4 7:54 a.m. SpaceShipOne re-enters the atmosphere, and the pilot feels five times the force of gravity.

5 8:12 a.m. SpaceShipOne touches down.

46,000 feet

1 6:48 a.m. ET SpaceShipOne is lifted off the runway by its carrier plane, White Knight.

Earth

Landing

Note: Times are unofficial.

Source: USA TODAY research

USA TODAY, 2004

Above: A test pilot celebrates on top of *SpaceShipOne*, the first spacecraft built and launched by a private company. Many people think that private space exploration is the wave of the future.

licensed from Rutan's company. Branson says operations will begin in about five years.

These entrepreneurs are proving that NASA-scale budgets aren't required. Though the exact cost of Rutan's project has not been revealed, Microsoft co-founder Paul Allen invested more than $20 million—a tiny number by NASA's standards.

The main market for these private spacecraft? Tourism. A market analysis three years ago by the firm Space Adventures concluded that at $100,000 per ticket, more than 10,000 people per year would purchase a trip on a suborbital spaceflight.

The one problem that has held back the dreams of these visionaries is that space travel has been too expensive for any entity but governments to indulge in. It looks now as though a few small groups of entrepreneurs are about to solve that problem.

When this movement comes to fruition, the age of commercial, low-cost space travel will affect our civilization in profound and unpredictable ways, as did commercial, low-cost aviation a century ago.

—Mark R. Whittington

WHO SHOULD PAY?

One of the hottest debates surrounding space exploration is the question of who should foot the bill. The United States has long been the world leader in space exploration. Is that a title it should strive to hold, or is it better to let other nations bear some of the burden of exploration? Or should exploration be left to private industry? U.S. planners have outlined four options:

1. The U.S. government should pay the full cost of U.S.-only space missions, just as it did with the Apollo missions.
2. The United States should foster international cooperation—and share costs—on collective space missions, as it did with the International Space Station.
3. The United States should offer financial incentives to private industry to encourage space exploration.
4. The United States should not pay for space exploration in any way.

The first of these scenarios is sometimes called the JFK (John F. Kennedy) model. In this model, space exploration is considered critical to the future of the United States and something the nation should pursue on its own. Proponents of this model suggest that international cooperation would leave the United States with little or no control over space missions. And if there's money to be made off Mars or the Moon, the United States might not get its fair share from an international effort. But opponents of this model argue that the United States can no longer afford to go it alone. The JFK model is too large a burden on U.S. taxpayers, they say.

In the second model, the United States would foster a consortium (group) of nations working together for a common goal. This model follows the approach taken in building the International Space Station. The benefits of this model are that no single country would have to bear the entire financial burden of a mission. The risks—as well as the benefits—would be shared. Opponents point out that the United States—because of its large size and economy—would still likely be the largest contributor to the project, yet it wouldn't retain control of the mission.

In the third model, the United States would offer financial incentives, such as tax breaks, for private industry to explore space. Backers of this model argue that a government space program is the most expensive type. They note that government operations can involve massive and costly amounts of red tape (official procedures and paperwork). They say private industry can do the same jobs for a fraction of the cost. But opponents note that private industry is unlikely to undertake space exploration purely for national pride or the glory of discovery. Industry will want a return on its investment, such as the right to set up mining operations on the Moon. And the idea of private companies exploiting something as

inspirational and beloved as the Moon is disturbing to some people.

Finally, some people believe the U.S. government should not spend any resources on space exploration. Their reasons are varied. Some simply want to reduce taxes as much as possible—they're in favor of cutting many kinds of government spending. Others believe that tax money should go to more immediate concerns, such as housing and feeding the poor, improving education, and fighting terrorism. Others simply see no value in space exploration.

WHAT'S THE PAYOFF?

For some, the idea of exploring and possibly colonizing another world is its own reward. The very act of scientific discovery would make such a mission worthwhile, they say. But others consider any money spent on space exploration to be an investment, and they expect a return on that investment. Is crewed exploration of other worlds an economic dead end, or will it provide real benefits to people back on Earth?

For those who see exploration as its own reward, Mars is often the preferred target. Landing astronauts on the Red Planet would net massive amounts of scientific data. Researchers could learn about the formation of the solar system, the chemistry of another world, and much more. There's even a chance they could discover Martian life, which would rank among the greatest scientific discoveries of all time. Some of the knowledge gained on a Mars mission might be valuable to industry. But any material wealth—such as metal ores—found on Mars would be impractical to send back to Earth. That's because the cost of transporting materials through space is so high. Even blocks of pure gold would cost more to transport from Mars than they'd be worth back on Earth.

The Moon is more appealing to those who see space exploration as a means to an end. The Moon's closeness to Earth could, in theory, make exploration profitable. Former astronaut Harrison H. Schmitt wrote the book *Return to the Moon: Exploration, Enterprise, and Energy in the Human*

> **❝ There is no evidence whatsoever that there is anything worth having out there [in space]. Even if the Moon was carpeted with diamonds, it would not be worth it because diamonds are not expensive enough [to offset the costs of shipping them back to Earth]. ❞**
>
> **—HEINZ WOLFF,** PROFESSOR OF BIOENGINEERING AND HONORARY MEMBER OF THE EUROPEAN SPACE AGENCY, 1999

Asteroid Mines

For acquiring mineral resources from space, asteroids might be our best bet. Scientists aren't entirely sure which materials make up most asteroids. But evidence suggests that at least some asteroids are rich in metals, including iron and nickel. Some asteroids may even have deposits of precious metals such as silver and gold.

Settlement of Space. In it, he argues that energy production could be the key payoff of Moon development. With energy resources on Earth dwindling and costs skyrocketing, alternative sources of energy will be a must in the future. Harrison believes that the Moon could help solve this looming crisis.

The Moon has rich supplies of hydrogen and helium. Nuclear power plants on the Moon could use both elements to create vast amounts of energy for use on Earth. Others imagine vast farms of solar cells on the surface of the Moon. These cells would use the Sun's rays to make power. Scientists have several ideas about how this energy could be transmitted back to Earth. The most popular is to send the energy as microwaves, which could be converted into electricity on Earth.

GOING PRIVATE

To many analysts, the idea of letting private companies bear the cost of space exploration makes the most sense. But private companies might be hesitant to invest in space with no guarantee that their investments will pay off. To make the idea more appealing to private business, U.S. lawmakers have put forth several proposals. In the mid-1990s, aerospace engineer and author Robert Zubrin and U.S. representative Newt Gingrich of Georgia proposed that the government offer cash incentives for companies willing to undertake Mars exploration.

The proposal included billions of dollars in cash prizes to anyone who could meet certain goals, such as putting a crew on Mars and returning them home safely. More recently, a bill called Zero G (gravity), Zero Tax would have given generous tax breaks to companies that invested in space exploration, but the bill never made it into law. Lawmakers have also proposed easing complicated and costly government regulations on space exploration to make it more affordable for private businesses.

Even with financial incentives, private business might be hesitant to undertake space exploration. It's true that developing industry beyond Earth, such as mining or energy production, might be extremely profitable. The problem is that the economic payoffs would be very long term. It could easily take decades for a business to see a return on its investment in space industry. Most people, businesses, and even nations are unwilling to spend vast amounts of money knowing that the return on their investment is so far off.

The Sell Mars Approach

Some people have suggested paying for a Mars mission by actually selling off plots of Martian land. Under this plan, people would pay for allotments of land, and all the money collected would pay for a crewed mission to the Red Planet. And in the future, if Mars colonization (settlement) takes off, buyers— or their descendants—would have the right to use or settle the Martian land. The biggest question with this approach is whether enough people would be willing to pay for land that they would be unlikely to ever visit in their lifetimes.

Moon 2.0

In 2007 the Internet search engine Google announced the Lunar X Prize, often called Moon 2.0. The competition is designed to promote private space exploration. The $20 million prize (along with bonuses) will go to the first privately funded team to successfully launch a spacecraft to the Moon, land on the surface, send a robot across the surface, and return images and data to Earth. As of 2011, twenty teams from around the world were in the running for the prize.

An earlier competition was the Ansari X Prize, which was funded by several private companies. This contest offered $10 million to the first private team to build and launch a reusable spacecraft. In 2004 the prize went to a company called Scaled Composites for the successful spaceflight of a craft called *SpaceShipOne*.

WHO SHOULD GO?

If a mission to Mars or the Moon were approved, how many astronauts should go? A high number of people would maximize the amount of research and exploration that could be done. Such maximization would be especially important for a Mars journey because of the great distance and high cost of the trip. So if we can afford only one trip to Mars, we should probably make the most of it and send as many astronauts as we can.

On the other hand, it would be relatively easy to make multiple trips to the Moon, so small crews might make more sense there. The Apollo missions sent three crew members, two of whom went to the surface. A similar crew arrangement could work again on the Moon.

Sending a large crew, especially to Mars, comes with serious downsides. The size—and cost—of a spacecraft goes up with each astronaut sent. With a large crew, living quarters would have to be bigger. Water, food, air, and other supply demands rise with each additional crew member. A larger, more fully loaded ship would require extra fuel, raising costs even further. And of course, the more people who go, the more lives are at risk. So what's the right number?

In his book *The Case for Mars*, Robert Zubrin suggests a crew of four. He says a Mars flight should have two flight engineers, or mechanics, who would be responsible for keeping the spacecraft working. Two field scientists—a geologist and a biochemist—would do the research and exploration for the mission. This small crew would keep down costs while still allowing for adequate scientific study. Each crew member would be cross-trained, or able to do multiple tasks. The mechanics would get scientific training. The field scientists would have a basic knowledge of how the spacecraft worked. One of the field scientists might get some medical training, since this scenario does not call for a separate medical officer. Each crew member would have to have a specialty as well as more general skills. That's the only way a small crew would work.

The issue of staffing becomes even more complicated in an international effort to go to Mars. On a joint mission involving several countries, it's likely that many or all participating nations would want representation aboard the spacecraft. Which astronaut and nation would get the honor of being the first to step foot on Mars? Which astronaut would be in command of the mission? Which language would the astronauts speak? Political questions such as these could easily increase the crew size—and the cost.

ONE-WAY TICKET?

A major part of the cost for any crewed Mars mission comes not from getting astronauts to Mars but from getting them home. A spacecraft would have to carry enough fuel to get the crew, their vehicle, and their gear down to the Martian surface, back up again, and home to Earth. That's a lot of fuel, and fuel is heavy. The more weight a spacecraft carries, the more expensive the trip will be. In addition, any craft designed to lift off Mars's surface would need all new technologies for doing so. Like Earth, Mars has a significant gravitational pull. A spacecraft must have powerful rockets to escape that pull. We have launchpads and other equipment for launching spacecraft here on Earth. But such infrastructure wouldn't be available on Mars. A Mars mission would have to rely on yet undeveloped technology for leaving the planet. Researching, building, and testing such technology would be one of the biggest expenses of such a mission.

For this reason, some have suggested slashing costs by eliminating the return trip. Under this controversial model, the trip to Mars would be one way. The crew would spend the rest of their lives on Mars. Former NASA engineer James C. McLane has promoted just such a plan. "When we eliminate the need to launch off Mars, we remove the mission's most daunting obstacle," he said. "Huge engineering challenges remain, but without a Mars launch, we can reasonably expect to devise a program that may be accomplished within the scope of current technology."

Under McLane's model, the crew would arrive with everything they needed to construct a habitat and survive on Mars. Even then, the harsh, unforgiving conditions on Mars and the difficulties of sending timely help from Earth would make the odds of their long-term survival grim. Could the U.S. public support sending its space heroes on a one-way trip?

IS A HUMAN CREW EVEN NECESSARY?

Automated spacecraft have visited every planet in the solar system and many of their moons. Robots equipped with cameras and other sensors have crawled around the surface of Mars and sent back vast amounts of data. These data have allowed scientists to study rocks, soil, and atmospheric conditions on Mars without even leaving Earth.

As the field of robotics continues to advance, we can do more and more with robotic spacecraft. Robot explorers can be our eyes and ears in space. Because they don't need to breathe air and don't need protection from deadly radiation, robots can go places where humans cannot. Perhaps most important, they can do so for a fraction of the cost that a crewed mission would require. For example, 2004 estimates for the cost of a crewed Mars mission were about $450 to $500 billion. Meanwhile, the cost of sending the rovers *Spirit* and *Opportunity* to Mars was around $900 million—about 2 percent of the cost of the proposed crewed mission. Thus, for the cost of a single crewed mission to Mars or the Moon, we could send dozens—possibly even hundreds—of robotic probes and rovers to gather data about the entire solar system. Many people believe that this is the best way to explore other worlds.

"Anything we want to do in space, we can do now more effectively, more efficiently and surely more safely with automated spacecraft," says former

Below: This image, made with a computer, shows what the *Spirit* rover looked like on the surface of Mars. *Spirit* traveled to Mars in 2004 and sent back data to Earth until 2010.

NASA historian Alex Roland. "There's no reason to be sending people to either the Moon or Mars."

While most people agree that robot explorers have their place, some believe they are no substitutes for human beings. The argument is that people can understand and adapt to what they find. They can conduct far more detailed and focused research than robots can. Crewed missions may be expensive, but they might also be infinitely more fruitful than robotic missions. Proponents of crewed space travel feel that if human beings ever intend to settle worlds beyond Earth, there's only one way to do it: board a spacecraft and go. It may be expensive, but many believe the effort would be well worth the cost.

"The human thirst for knowledge ultimately cannot be satisfied by even the most vivid pictures or the most detailed measurements," President Bush said in 2004. "We need to see and examine and touch for ourselves, and only human beings are capable of adapting to the inevitable uncertainties posed by space travel."

CHAPTER FOUR

Risky Business: The Dangers of Space Exploration

BY THE 1980S, PUBLIC INTEREST IN NASA AND THE U.S. space program had fallen off. The space shuttle program was in full swing, but it generated little excitement. After all, the shuttles weren't going anywhere spectacular such as the Moon. All they did was go into orbit and then return to Earth. Shuttle launches had started to seem routine. To many, sending a shuttle into space just wasn't that exciting.

In 1986 all that changed. NASA was working hard to rekindle the public's interest in the space program. It began a program to train ordinary civilians and send them into space. In 1985 NASA had selected high school social studies teacher Christa McAuliffe of Concord, New Hampshire, to be the first teacher in space. NASA planned to have McAuliffe broadcast science lessons from the orbiting shuttle to schools across the nation.

Left: The world was excited when high school teacher Christa McAuliffe *(front)* joined the *Challenger* space shuttle crew in 1986. But when the shuttle exploded shortly after launch, excitement turned to shock and grief.

McAuliffe and her six astronaut crewmates boarded the shuttle *Challenger* at Kennedy Space Center on the morning of January 28, 1986. McAuliffe's presence had indeed heightened interest in the shuttle program. Many people—especially schoolchildren—were tuned in to watch the launch on TV.

The countdown reached zero, and the shuttle's rocket boosters fired. A huge plume of smoke billowed around the shuttle as it began to rise. Viewers watched as *Challenger* climbed higher and higher.

Nobody knew it until that point, but the shuttle had a problem. Normally, small seals called O-rings kept rocket fuel from seeping out of the shuttle's rocket boosters. But one of *Challenger*'s O-rings was no longer doing its job. Hot gases were seeping out of the booster. As *Challenger* climbed into the sky, the gases caught fire and spread along the outside of the craft's fuel tank. The tank wasn't built to withstand that kind of heat. About seventy-three seconds after launch, viewers watched in horror as *Challenger* broke apart in the sky. Long trails of smoke hung in the air as the remains of *Challenger* fell back to Earth. All seven crew members, including Christa McAuliffe, died in the accident.

The explosion of *Challenger* served as a sobering reminder. Space travel is never routine. Astronauts are always one mistake or one malfunction away from disaster. This danger will be ever present in any missions to the Moon or Mars.

The *Challenger* disaster came as a result of a part failure. But that's just one of the dangers to astronauts traveling to another world. Among the many dangers astronauts face would include human error; deadly radiation from the Sun and from deep space; the harsh, unforgiving conditions of another world; and the effects of zero gravity (no gravity) on the human body.

THE THREAT OF MALFUNCTION

As the *Challenger* disaster showed, one of the most dangerous times for any space mission comes at takeoff. At takeoff, engines and rocket boosters

Above: As the world watched on television in 1986, *Challenger* exploded in the sky above the Atlantic Ocean. The event demonstrated the dangers of space exploration.

must successfully control the burning of thousands of pounds of explosive rocket fuel. Spacecraft need rockets to escape the pull of Earth's gravity. But as with *Challenger*, the smallest mistake or malfunction during takeoff can result in catastrophe.

Reentry—or returning to Earth from space—can be another deadly time for a spacecraft. A spacecraft's heat shield is designed to protect the craft and crew from the blistering heat created during descent through Earth's atmosphere. The heat comes from friction—the rubbing of the craft against the atmosphere as it descends. In 2003, unknown to astronauts or mission controllers, the shuttle *Columbia*'s heat shield was damaged shortly after liftoff. During reentry, heat penetrated the damaged heat shield, entered the shuttle's wing, and destroyed the wing. As a result of this damage, the shuttle broke apart as it neared the ground. All seven crew members were killed.

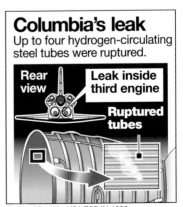

Columbia's leak
Up to four hydrogen-circulating steel tubes were ruptured.

Rear view

Leak inside third engine

Ruptured tubes

By Gary Visgaitis, USA TODAY, 1999
Source: NASA, AP

Grieving Americans See Profound Mission; Exploration of Space Still Vital, Most Say

<u>From the Pages of</u> <u>USA TODAY</u> A nation still recovering from the terror attacks of 2001 and bracing for war with Iraq tried Sunday to cope with the loss of seven explorers whose names and mission became familiar only in tragedy.

But across much of the country, reaction to the *Columbia* disaster was somewhat muted, partly because Americans have become more aware of the danger of space travel. A USA TODAY/CNN/Gallup Poll taken Sunday found that 71% of Americans said they had thought that sooner or later such a spaceflight disaster would occur again. Still, 94% said they were deeply or somewhat upset.

A day after the space shuttle tore apart en route to landing, airline pilots asked their passengers to observe a moment of silence and pastors asked their parishioners to observe the frailty of life. Flowers piled up at the dead astronauts' high schools and on the grave of Christa McAuliffe, who died along with six other astronauts when the *Challenger* exploded in 1986.

Once again, people pondered the cost of mankind's age-old quest to explore what President Bush called "the darkness beyond our world."

The cost of exploration has been constant, for Magellan in 1521 in the Philippines and for McAuliffe, who would have been the first teacher in space. But most Americans say the quest must go on.

In the USA TODAY/CNN/Gallup Poll, 82% said they wanted manned space shuttle flights to continue; only 15% did not. Similarly, 80% supported the same or increased spending on the U.S. space program; 16% thought space funds should be cut or ceased. The poll has a margin of error of plus or minus 5 percentage points.

Success had made some regard a shuttle flight as routine as a cross-town bus trip.

But in their grief and shock, Americans seemed to see such missions less as scientific expeditions than as something more profound—"our building of pyramids," in the words of Paul Chaikin, a Princeton University [New Jersey] physicist.

In Houston [Texas], hundreds of people gathered at Grace Community Church, not far from the Johnson Space Center, to remember fellow parishioners and *Columbia* astronauts Rick Husband and Michael Anderson.

"We cannot understand why these things happen, but there was a purpose in Rick's life, and that purpose is being filled," said Russell Naisbitt, a friend of Husband's.

A few miles away, at the main gate to the space center, hundreds of people visited a makeshift shrine, dropping off bouquets, candles, signs, American and Israeli flags, stuffed animals and balloons.

At Indian River City United Methodist Church, children released seven gold balloons—one for each life lost. "Something we were part of went terribly wrong," the Rev. Jim Govatos said.

—Rick Hampson, Charisse Jones, and Rita Rubin

Above: Astronaut David Brown, who died when the space shuttle *Columbia* broke apart, is buried with military honors at Arlington National Cemetery in Virginia in 2003.

Everyone involved with the space program, especially the astronauts, knows these dangers. At the time of the *Columbia* disaster, NASA estimated the odds of a catastrophic failure with any single shuttle mission—and certain death for any astronaut—to be 1 in 150.

DEADLY RADIATION

Space may look empty, but in truth, it's filled with energy, including deadly radiation. Even our own Sun emits harmful radiation. While we're on Earth, the atmosphere and Earth's magnetic field—an invisible zone of magnetic force—protect us from most of this radiation. But the radiation bombards everything out in space.

Dangerous radiation includes ultraviolet rays, X-rays, gamma rays, and cosmic rays. Such radiation can rip apart human cells from the inside out. Large doses of radiation can kill almost immediately. Smaller doses can cause people to develop deadly cancers later in life. Other health problems from radiation include cataracts, or a clouding of the lenses in the eyes, and reduced fertility rates—or reduced chances of having children.

Mars and the Moon do not have magnetic fields to protect astronauts from radiation. Mars has only a thin atmosphere to provide protection, and the Moon doesn't have any atmosphere. So astronauts on Mars or the Moon would be exposed to

> **We estimated our odds of not coming back [to Earth] at 1 in 70. Those are not very good odds. It only gets worse as you go further out [into space].**
>
> **—JOHN GRUNSFELD,**
> U.S. ASTRONAUT, ON THE DANGERS OF A 2009 SPACE WALK

dangerous radiation. But even worse radiation exposure would come during space travel. Even though spacecraft have radiation shielding, astronauts in space are bombarded by radiation from all sides. One study estimated that one in ten astronauts involved in a mission to Mars would develop cancer as a result of exposure to radiation in space. John Swigert, the pilot of *Apollo 13*, died of cancer. So did Walter Schirra, commander of *Apollo 7*. There's no way to know whether their time in space caused these cancers, but it's certainly possible.

Scientists say that female astronauts, because their breasts and reproductive organs are especially susceptible to cancers, are under greater danger from radiation than male astronauts. For this reason, a crewed mission to Mars might include only male astronauts. Better radiation shielding in spacecraft could help protect crews. Faster rockets that can shorten a crew's travel time—and thus their exposure to radiation—might be the best protection.

HARSH ENVIRONMENTS

Once they reached the surface of the Moon or Mars, astronauts would face a whole new set of problems. People are built to survive on Earth. We are physically suited to Earth's atmosphere, temperature, and gravity. On the Moon or Mars, all this changes. Humans aren't built to survive in these worlds. Living on Mars or the Moon would involve a constant struggle to overcome a harsh environment.

Earth has a thick atmosphere, rich in oxygen and usually at a temperature human beings can tolerate. The weight of the atmosphere pressing down on Earth is called atmospheric pressure, or air pressure. Our bodies are built to live at a certain pressure. Too much pressure and the atmosphere would crush us. Too little and our bodies wouldn't be able to hold in any air or fluids. The Moon, on the other hand, has no atmosphere and no atmospheric pressure. The astronauts who walked on the Moon in the 1960s and 1970s wore pressurized space suits, equipped with oxygen tanks. Future Moon visitors would have to do the same or would have to live in sealed, airtight environments at all times.

Outer Space without a Suit

Sometimes astronauts must leave their spacecraft to make repairs on satellites or a space station. When they do, they wear heavy-duty space suits. The suits protect them from the inhospitable environment of outer space. Space suits maintain a comfortable temperature and pressure. They supply astronauts with oxygen. They block out harmful radiation from space. They even protect astronauts from small, ultrafast bits of dust that could otherwise harm them.

What would happen if you went into space without a suit? You wouldn't last long. The lack of air pressure would cause water in your cells to turn to water vapor, or gas. Your entire body would begin to swell. All the air would be sucked out of your lungs, and you would start to suffocate. Scientists say that a person without protection in space would lose consciousness in about nine to twelve seconds and die in about ninety seconds.

Above: U.S. astronaut Michael Good does maintenance work on the exterior of the International Space Station. If he didn't wear a space suit, he would be dead in less than two minutes.

Mars does have an atmosphere, but it's a fraction the thickness of Earth's atmosphere. Therefore, Mars's atmospheric pressure is far too low for human bodies. In addition, humans couldn't breathe the air on Mars, because the atmosphere doesn't have enough oxygen. As with the Moon, human travelers to Mars would have to be protected by space suits or would have to live in sealed environments.

Temperatures on Mars and the Moon are also inhospitable. Mars is always cold, with an average temperature around −67°F (−55°C). The Moon's temperature swings wildly. During the night, temperatures on the Moon can dip to almost −400°F (−240°C). At noon temperatures on the Moon can soar to more than 250°F (121°C). Humans could not survive on either Mars or the Moon without special protection from extreme temperatures.

Both Mars and the Moon are smaller than Earth, so they have less gravity. Without the strong pull of gravity, humans don't need to use their muscles as much. For instance, when astronauts walked on the Moon, just the slightest physical effort sent them bounding over the surface. This might look like fun, but when we don't use our muscles, they become weak. Even the human heart muscle can become weakened without enough gravity.

Below: Gravity doesn't affect astronauts in orbit the same way it affects people on Earth. This astronaut aboard the ISS floats because gravity isn't pulling him down.

In space, astronauts experience almost no gravity, a condition called microgravity. Scientists aren't sure how microgravity would affect the human body over long periods—for instance, over the course of a long space voyage or space settlement. Scientists have observed loss of bone density and muscle tone in people who have lived aboard the International Space Station. Astronauts there must spend hours a day doing strenuous exercise to keep their muscles toned. The same would be true for people on Mars or the Moon.

ARE THE DANGERS TOO GREAT?

Are the risks of crewed travel to Mars or the Moon worthwhile?

Some people don't think so. Human life is too valuable, they say. Sending people to the Moon or Mars could end up being a death sentence. Technology has come a long way in recent decades. Robots can do our exploring for us, many people argue. Why risk human lives when technology can do many of the same jobs?

Proponents of crewed exploration disagree. Human beings are explorers, some argue. Curiosity and the quest for knowledge are in our blood. Yes, sending people to Mars or the Moon comes with serious risks. But risk is simply a part of exploration. After all, in the 1400s and 1500s, when Europeans boarded ships and sailed across

> **We understand the risks that are involved in human spaceflight, and we know that these risks are manageable. But we also know that they're serious and can have deadly consequences.**
>
> **—RON DITTEMORE,**
> NASA SPACE SHUTTLE PROGRAM MANAGER, 2003

the Atlantic Ocean to North America, they were taking massive risks. Many ships were lost at sea. Many people caught incurable diseases along the way. Food supplies were often inadequate. Yet people willingly took those risks. Proponents of crewed spaceflight believe that this spirit of exploration is still alive and part of us and that sending people to other worlds is the next logical step.

Americans seem to agree. A 2008 Gallup Poll revealed that 68 percent of Americans believe that the benefits of crewed space exploration outweighed the risks. Another Gallup Poll showed that if given the chance, 59 percent of teens aged thirteen to seventeen would like to travel to the Moon someday. About 48 percent of teens said they'd like to be the first person on Mars.

CHAPTER FIVE

Stir Crazy: The Psychological Risks of Space Travel

IN JUNE 2010, SIX MEN UNDERTOOK A JOURNEY TO Mars—without ever leaving Moscow, Russia. In truth, the journey was just a simulation (pretend) flight called Mars 500. Researchers weren't interested in testing rockets, scientific sensors, or other equipment involved with a real voyage. They really wanted to know how, on a simulated flight of 520 days, the crew would respond to being closed in and isolated from the world.

The experiment, conducted at the Institute of Biomedical Problems in Moscow, calls attention to a problem often overlooked with crewed spaceflight— the state of astronauts' mental health. With current technology, astronauts on a mission to Mars might be gone for years. The same would be true for astronauts stationed on a Moon base. How would such an extended stay in space affect them mentally?

Left: If six astronauts were to travel through space for a year and a half, how would they cope? To help researchers find out, six men *(four of them shown at left)* signed on to Mars 500, a simulated 520-day spaceflight.

To find out, on June 28, 2010, six men—three Russian, one French, one Italian, and one Chinese—said farewell to the world and locked themselves inside a simulated spacecraft, about the size of a small apartment, lacking even windows. The men planned to spend the next 520 days—about a year and a half—there. They came from different cultures. They spoke different languages, although all had at least a basic knowledge of English, which enabled them to communicate with one another. Inside the "spacecraft," they were subjected to many of the stresses and tasks a real Mars crew might face. The mission consisted of a 250-day simulated outbound flight, a 30-day stay on a simulated Mars (complete with excursions onto a fake Martian surface), and a 240-day return trip. The men shared five rooms, ate prepackaged food, and showered only once every ten days. Many suggested that the crew would be begging to be released long before their mission was completed.

The point of the experiment wasn't to be cruel. And while it may sound like the plot of the next reality TV show, it was actually serious business. Researchers wanted to gauge what happens to social order and to the human mind under such circumstances. Can a crew even make it to Mars without going crazy or turning on one another? Those are the kinds of questions researchers hoped to answer.

The Moscow experiment wasn't the first of its kind. In 2000 a crew of six endured a similar simulated mission for eight months. This mission included four men and two women, and the mix proved problematic. The time in isolation caused at least one of the men to become aggressive toward the women. Threats grew into violence. One of the women locked herself away in a room to escape. Some blamed these problems on the inclusion of alcohol in the crew quarters. Others just blamed human nature.

Many people question whether such simulations are even valid. The simulations may reproduce certain conditions that a real crew would face, but many things would be different. A crew aboard a spacecraft on a real mission to Mars would have to live with the knowledge of constant danger. The level of stress would be higher—as would the level of anxiety, fear, and excitement about reaching another world. These factors could fundamentally change how people respond.

Still, the Moscow crew believed in the importance of their experiment. "When people say this is a simulation, that it isn't a matter of life and death, I tell them it's much more," said Wang Yue, the Chinese crew member. "It's the future of mankind."

A CLOSED SYSTEM

By nature, human beings are social creatures. We thrive on interactions with other people. We enjoy socializing with friends and family in person, on the phone, and via the Internet. But astronauts on long-term missions would live in closed and very limited social systems. They would have only one another to personally interact and socialize with. E-mail would be possible, as would

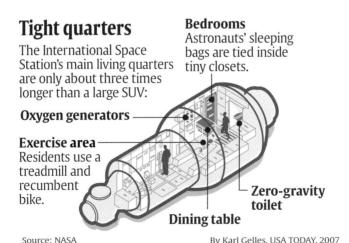

Tight quarters

The International Space Station's main living quarters are only about three times longer than a large SUV:

Oxygen generators

Exercise area
Residents use a treadmill and recumbent bike.

Bedrooms
Astronauts' sleeping bags are tied inside tiny closets.

Zero-gravity toilet

Dining table

Source: NASA   By Karl Gelles, USA TODAY, 2007

> **" If astronauts were on Mars, hundreds of millions of miles away from Earth, with up to 44 minutes of delayed communication between themselves and mission control, they would really feel isolated. You couldn't send them surprise packages or supplies. If someone had a medical emergency, you couldn't evacuate them home. How would astronauts deal with such conditions? "**
>
> **—NICK KANAS,** PROFESSOR OF PSYCHIATRY
> AT THE UNIVERSITY OF CALIFORNIA, SAN FRANCISCO, 2009

some radio contact with Earth. But as a spacecraft moves farther and farther from Earth, it takes radio waves longer and longer to travel back and forth. So traditional, spoken conversation would be all but impossible.

And what if crew members didn't get along? They would be constantly exposed to one another, with no real way to avoid those they didn't like. Imagine being locked in a windowless hotel room with someone you couldn't stand—for a year and a half or longer. There would be no escape. Disagreements could turn into arguments, which could lead to outright hostility. Personal conflicts could even turn violent.

NASA acknowledged this problem in a 2002 report. The report said, "Schisms [divisions], friction, withdrawal, competitiveness, scapegoating, and other maladaptive [negative] group behaviors are found among highly competent men and women working together in normal settings. They can also be expected among astronaut crews."

Studies have shown that astronauts often experience a condition called displacement. When problems arise on a mission, they don't focus their anger on themselves or their crewmates but rather on mission control staff back on Earth. Nick Kanas, a psychiatry professor and leading researcher in the field of astronaut psychology, explained: "When a group of people are under stress...they may redirect their frustrations onto people outside the group. That's displacement. And for the astronauts, they redirected their tension onto mission-control personnel."

Above: Six astronauts prepare to board the space shuttle *Discovery* in early 2011. On short space shuttle flights, astronauts usually get along well. But what would happen if they were cooped up together for many months?

Over the short term, such displacement usually results in little more than some strained working relationships between those in the spacecraft and those on Earth. But over a long mission, anger with mission control could turn to distrust, which could potentially undermine the mission.

The mixing of genders on a crew and the potential for sexual tension could complicate matters further. Both men and women can become competitive and even aggressive in the presence of the opposite sex. Would mixing genders on a long space mission invite social disharmony, or could a highly trained crew manage any sexual tension for the duration of the mission? Would crews need to be limited to one gender, or would a group of committed romantic couples provide the most stable social structure? In the latter scenario, how might the crew be affected if two or more crew members cheated on their partners? How might that impact the ability of the crew to work toward a common goal?

MENTAL HEALTH

Another question concerns the psychological stresses that a crew would face on a long mission. Psychologists define spaceflight as an isolated, confined, and extreme (ICE) environment—an environment so stressful that the development of psychological problems of some degree is highly probable. Such problems for a crew, especially in a Mars mission, could range from prolonged boredom to intense claustrophobia (fear of being in small spaces) to outright psychosis—or a mental break with reality. Of course, any crew would undergo intense psychological screening ahead of time, which NASA already does. Anyone who shows tendancies toward psychological problems is quickly eliminated from the astronaut program. However, even NASA has admitted that its screening procedures are imperfect.

> **" In terms of the astronauts facing stresses, I don't believe the stress response would be dissimilar to other high-stress organizations. . . . We prepare astronauts not only through training but also through their medical evaluations to face those stresses. "**
>
> **—JEFF DAVIS,**
> NASA'S DIRECTOR OF SPACE LIFE SCIENCES, 2007

Claustrophobia would also disqualify any prospective astronaut. For all practical purposes, a person who is aware of having claustrophobia is unlikely to pursue spaceflight in the first place. However, phobias can develop at any point in life. And more than a year of confinement in an extremely small space—no more than a few hundred square feet— might induce some degree of claustrophobia, even in someone who hadn't previously experienced it.

Depression—a state of long-term sadness and despair—is another potentially serious side effect of space travel. Astronauts on a Mars mission would be removed from friends and family. Their normal support systems would be gone. If depression set in, a crew member's performance could be severely impaired. Many people suffering from depression take on an attitude of pessimism or defeatism. On a spacecraft, where the peak performance of every crew member might be the difference between success and failure—even life or death—such an attitude could pose a risk to all involved.

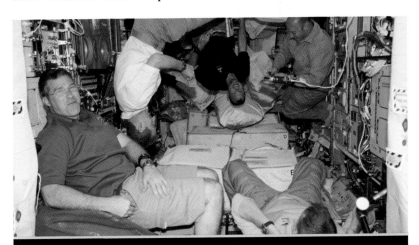

Above: These crew members aboard the ISS live in cramped quarters for months at a time. Any spacecraft traveling to Mars would probably be even more cramped and the voyage could take close to two years.

Insomnia in Space

Human beings sleep for about one-third of their lives—about eight hours in each twenty-four-hour day. Sleep is critical to proper mental and physical functioning. But space travel and low- or zero-gravity environments can seriously hamper astronauts' ability to get enough sleep. Many astronauts have reported insomnia (inability to sleep) in space. That's because the human body isn't built for zero-gravity sleep. In a spacecraft, you can't easily lie down and curl up under the covers. Your blanket and pillow will simply float away from you. Some space shuttle astronauts use Velcro straps to attach themselves to their beds and bedding *(below)*. Others simply sleep while floating through the spacecraft—upright, upside down, or in another position. Many just can't get a good night's sleep.

Insomnia can harm mental function, and if the insomnia is prolonged, the problem grows and grows. Insomnia could be a big obstacle on a long-term space mission. If astronauts are already in a high-stress environment, adding insomnia to the mix could speed up the onset of psychological problems.

And of course, the stresses of long-term space travel could bring on even more serious psychological problems, such as psychosis. In a state of psychosis, people lose clarity in their mental processes. Their connection with reality begins to erode. Some grow distant. Others hear voices in their heads or imagine events that never happened.

What would a Mars crew do if someone became delusional in this way? NASA has actually created guidelines for such a situation. They call for other crew members to bind the individual at the wrists and the ankles with duct tape and secure him or her to a wall with bungee cords. Crew members can also inject the delusional person with tranquilizing drugs if necessary. These measures might suffice for a near-Earth flight of a few days, but what about a mission of several years? Would a delusional individual have to be restrained all that time? Would the mission have to be aborted? Medical treatment would be virtually impossible in such a situation. There's no easy answer.

Many consider the risk of such psychosis to be minimal. After all, they say, astronauts are healthy, hardworking, and extensively educated. But that doesn't prevent the onset of mental instability. Consider the case of former NASA astronaut Lisa Nowak. Like all astronauts, Nowak was highly educated and had been thoroughly screened by NASA. She served as a mission specialist aboard a July 2006 shuttle flight. Half a year later, she was under arrest for attempting to kidnap the girlfriend of astronaut William Oefelein. Nowak had somehow become fixated on Oefelein and wanted to remove his girlfriend, whom she viewed as a rival for his romantic affections.

The case of Lisa Nowak is the exception, not the rule. But it demonstrates that astronauts are only human and that they come with all the failings of humans. If people can crack under the normal stresses of life on Earth, what might happen to them under the stresses of life in space?

The Price of Obsession

From the Pages of
USA TODAY

Just how much pressure does it take for a person to snap—to abandon reason, family, the entire structure of their life in a desperate emotional quest for the unattainable?

Whatever it is, the bizarre tale of Lisa Nowak *(below)*, stellar astronaut turned stalker and perhaps would-be killer, seems to suggest that virtually no one is immune. Nowak, 43, was high school valedictorian, with the right stuff to join NASA. She flew on a space shuttle mission just seven months ago and posed with President Bush—all while mothering three children.

Yet Nowak veered so far off course Monday that Hollywood would be hard-pressed to add to the drama. She reportedly became so intensely jeal-

ous of a younger competitor for the affections of NASA shuttle pilot William Oefelein, 41, that she drove non-stop from Houston to Florida wearing diapers to avoid stopping. There, according to police, she executed a meticulously planned assault and is now accused of attempted murder.

The answer to the question—What made her snap?—may be unknowable. Perhaps it's enough to say that we are all human. Experts on jealousy agree that intelligent people aren't necessarily more skilled at emotions and relationships—even when they can discipline themselves to achieve such reach-for-the-stars ambitions as Nowak did. When stresses align to expose a person's deepest frailties, he or she may crack.

Nowak will need psychiatric help, which NASA seems inclined to provide. But as the drama unfolds, some good might be done if it focuses attention on one product of obsession: stalking. Some 1.4 million people, mostly women, are stalked annually in the USA, according to the National Center for Victims of Crime. Nowak is said to have stalked her victim for two months.

High-profile cases, including the 1989 murder of actress Rebecca Schaeffer, led to anti-stalking laws. But the crime is hard to prove and has grown with the Internet.

Nowak's story is unique, but what it reveals is not. Stalkers and their targets are both in need of attention.

—USA TODAY editors

CHAPTER SIX

The Final Frontier: Colonization and Terraforming

FOR MANY, THE QUESTION ABOUT SENDING A CREWED mission to the Moon or Mars isn't just one of exploration. They believe that travel to these worlds should end in inhabited Mars and Moon stations and bases, and eventually long-term Mars and Moon colonies.

The idea of spreading the human race to other worlds is appealing. After all, Earth has experienced many massive extinction events in its past—times when entire species have been wiped out by natural disasters. Some argue that by staying put on Earth, humanity is putting all its eggs in one basket. A nuclear war, an asteroid impact, or another catastrophe could wipe out human civilization with little or no warning. By spreading to the Moon and Mars, some say, humanity would increase its odds of surviving such a disaster.

Critics point out the difficulty of ever settling another world. Mars and the Moon are not hospitable places for human beings. The Moon does not have an

Left: An artist imagines what a futuristic human colony on Mars might look like.

> " We're human beings. We evolved to flourish in a very specific environment that covers perhaps 10 percent of our home planet's surface area. . . . Space itself is a very poor environment for humans to live in. A simple pressure failure can kill a spaceship crew in minutes. And that's not the only threat. Cosmic radiation poses a serious risk to long duration interplanetary missions. "

—CHARLES STROSS,
SCIENCE FICTION WRITER, 2007

atmosphere. It doesn't have easily accessible stores of water. Its surface temperature swings between extreme heat and extreme cold. It's possible that people could set up an underground base on the Moon—with food, air, and water shipped in from Earth. But such a settlement would always be reliant on Earth for resupply. It would not be a self-sustaining colony.

For this reason, most scientists consider Mars to be the more logical choice for a human colony. Mars is bigger than the

Moon. It has an atmosphere and water.

Still, starting a colony on Mars would be a daunting prospect. Yes, Mars has an atmosphere. But it is thin. The atmospheric pressure is too low for human survival, and the atmosphere provides little protection from harmful radiation. It also doesn't have the mixture of gases human beings need to breathe. Mars has water, but this water is frozen and difficult to access. And Mars is bitterly cold, even during Martian summers.

To overcome these problems, a Martian colony would probably have to start out underground, like a bunker. An underground structure would provide its inhabitants protection from radiation. The structure would have to be pressurized and airtight–keeping air and warmth in and the Martian cold out. People might also be able to build colonies under clear plastic domes, probably inside Mars's deepest canyons. Getting as low as possible would have many advantages. It would give inhabitants the highest possible amount of natural atmospheric pressure. And canyon walls would help protect the colony from radiation.

In theory, a Mars colony could be self-sustaining. Colonists could use machines to turn Mars's ice into liquid water and to extract oxygen from the Martian atmosphere. Colonists could then recycle the air and water. Colonists could also grow crops and other plants inside greenhouses. The colony could extract building materials, such as iron, from the ground. Solar panels or small nuclear power plants could provide energy.

Below: A Martian colony might include clear plastic spheres, with plants inside for creating oxygen and with living spaces for humans.

However, such a colony would be fragile. A structural failure in a dome or a bunker—one that allowed precious air to escape—could be a death sentence for the inhabitants. Any damage to a greenhouse, air recyclers, or water recyclers would also spell disaster. The colony would have no advanced medical facilities. If someone were seriously injured or sick, help from Earth would be months or even years away. Colonists would be engaged in a daily struggle for survival. Without regular resupply from Earth, their chances of long-term survival would be small.

TERRAFORMING MARS

Many scientists dream bigger when they think of the colonization of Mars. A series of small colonies scraping out a fragile existence on a cold, dead world isn't what they have in mind. They want to go to a planet that's ready to welcome humans with warm air and open skies.

But to build such a habitat, human beings would have to drastically alter the face of Mars. Colonists would have to terraform it—that is, alter its atmosphere and surface. The question of whether we could—or even should—undertake such a venture remains very much a matter of debate.

The first question about terraforming is whether it could be done. Present-day Mars is a cold and apparently lifeless world. To change this world, humans would have to make several major changes in Mars's atmosphere. First, the atmosphere would have to be made thicker and heavier. This would increase the planet's atmospheric pressure, making it suitable for human life, and would provide additional protection from harmful radiation. The atmosphere would also need to be warmed. It would need to reach temperatures high enough for liquid water to exist on the surface.

Scientists—and science fiction writers—have many ideas for bringing about these changes. The first step in any plan would be to heat the planet's surface.

As the planet grew hotter, ice and frozen gases trapped underground and at the Martian poles would begin to sublimate, or turn from solid into gas. With more gases, the atmosphere would thicken slowly over time. A thicker atmosphere would hold more heat from the Sun. The extra heat would cause more sublimation, and the cycle would continue.

We could start the heating process in several ways. Some scientists have suggested placing huge mirrors in orbit around Mars. The mirrors would reflect sunlight onto the Martian poles and heat them. Another plan is to dig deep holes into Mars's surface. The holes would allow heat trapped deep inside the planet to escape into its atmosphere. A third plan would be to add tiny organisms called microbes to the Martian surface. The microbes would produce methane, a greenhouse gas. In an atmosphere, greenhouse gases act like a blanket. They warm a planet by trapping the Sun's heat, preventing it from traveling back out into space.

NASA scientists have also suggested manufacturing greenhouse gases called perfluorocarbons (PFCs) on the Martian surface. These gases could be produced from raw materials already found on Mars. PFCs are ten thousand times more effective at trapping heat than carbon dioxide, the most common greenhouse gas on Earth. According to NASA, producing PFCs could create an initial temperature rise of 7.2°F (4°C) on Mars. This increase would start the cycle of heating and sublimation needed to further warm Mars's atmosphere. The final result would be a global temperature rise of 126°F (70°C).

Perhaps the most spectacular plan that has been proposed so far is to start terraforming by crashing an asteroid into Mars. From Earth, astronauts could travel to an asteroid and attach rockets to it. The astronauts would return home and the rockets would then guide the asteroid to Mars. The asteroid's impact would release tremendous amounts of heat into the atmosphere.

Once Mars has a thicker, warmer atmosphere, the next step would be introducing Earth-based life to the planet. Mars's atmosphere is rich in carbon dioxide, but it contains little oxygen, which humans need to breathe. But plants absorb carbon dioxide and produce oxygen, so we could send plants to Mars. Hardy strains of algae and lichens, which could survive the harsh Martian environment, might be the first to arrive. Larger plants could follow, along with insects to spread pollen (grains that enable plants to reproduce) from plant to plant. As plant life spreads, the atmosphere would grow richer and richer in oxygen. In time, people and animals could safely breathe the Martian air.

Most scientists who have studied the theories behind terraforming agree that it is possible, at least to some degree. After all, human activities—specifically the burning of coal, oil, and natural gas—have released

> 66 **Terraforming is very long-term . . . but it's a survival question. Sooner or later, I think a mature society owes it to the future to preserve this society by establishing a survivable place other than Earth. There's potential of life being there. When we get there, there will be life. We'll start growing things and Mars will be gradually supportive of human existence.** 99
>
> —**BUZZ ALDRIN,** FORMER APOLLO ASTRONAUT AND THE SECOND MAN ON THE MOON, 2009

greenhouse gases and warmed Earth's atmosphere significantly in the last hundred years. Some scientists say that Mars could be similarly terraformed in a matter of decades. Not everyone agrees on the timescale, however. Some scientists say it would take thousands of years before people could walk under an open Martian sky.

THE ETHICS OF TERRAFORMING

Changing a planet to suit human needs sounds like science fiction. But while many people get caught up in the question of how to do it, they sometimes forget the question of whether we *should* do it.

Author Alex Moore writes for Red Colony, a website that advocates exploration and colonization of Mars. He is in favor of terraforming, but he also points out the argument against it. "Terraforming is a huge undertaking," he explains. "When we speak of terraforming we speak of completely changing an entire planet's climate, geology, and life. We speak of destroying land masses and geological features billions of years old, of raising the global temperature tens of degrees, and flooding the surface with huge oceans. We speak of releasing thousands of species from another planet to live and breed, changing Mars' atmospheric composition with every breath."

Do we have the right to so completely reshape the face of another world? Perhaps if we knew that Mars was just a pile of dead rocks and dust, this would be a minor concern. But the possibility that life might already exist on Mars complicates the issue. Scientists have gathered some evidence that the Red Planet might already have life of its own. Martian life-forms, if they exist, are most likely microbes that are far too small to be seen with the naked eye. They might live deep beneath the planet's surface or under the polar ice caps.

If we knew Mars was home to its own life, would it be ethical to terraform? Such drastic changes to the planet's environment would very likely wipe out any life the planet already held. Even if the life on Mars was just microbes, would we be justified in killing an entire planetary life system just to give ourselves more space to live? Some argue that even without any evidence, we can never be sure that life doesn't exist on Mars. After all, scientists on Earth are still discovering life-forms in places where they never expected to find them, such as in superhot volcanic vents under the ocean. If we're still finding life on Earth, how could we ever eliminate the possibility of life on Mars? By terraforming the Red Planet, we'd run the risk of driving an entire planet's species into extinction.

THE BIOLOGICAL IMPERATIVE

Life on Earth is fragile. Sixty-five million years ago, millions of dinosaurs roamed the planet. Then a single asteroid slammed into Earth. The impact sent millions of

Above: Sixty-five million years ago, an asteroid strike wiped out much of the life on Earth, including dinosaurs. Some say we should colonize space before a similar disaster wipes out humanity.

tons of dust flying high into the atmosphere. The dust hung in the air for years, blocking out sunlight and drastically dropping global temperatures. Without sunlight, plants died. Without plants to eat, animals died. These animals included the dinosaurs, which soon became extinct.

Another asteroid impact, such as the one that wiped out the dinosaurs, could wipe out people. But humanity faces other threats as well. A war fought with nuclear weapons would also be deadly to almost all life on Earth. Nuclear bombs not only kill people and destroy buildings. They also release deadly radiation into the atmosphere. In addition, nuclear explosions would send tons of dust and debris into the atmosphere, again blocking out sunlight and leading to the death of plants and animals. More than twenty thousand nuclear weapons exist on Earth—more than enough to kill us all many times over. And if nuclear war didn't kill us, a terrible epidemic—or widespread outbreak of disease—could wipe out humanity.

Because of these threats and others, some people hold that human beings must colonize other worlds to ensure the survival of the human species. Scientist Carl Sagan explained, "Every surviving civilization is obliged to become spacefaring— not because of exploratory or romantic zeal [enthusiasm], but for the most practical reason imaginable: staying alive."

In the near term, the odds of the destruction of the human race are low. Over more than two million years, human beings have survived everything nature has thrown at us. But that doesn't mean we'll always be safe. Who knows what the next thousand or million years will bring. Having a self-sustaining colony on Mars would provide a sort of insurance policy against human extinction. If Earth suffered some terrible tragedy, the people on Mars would be there to make sure the human species survived. Having a Mars colony might also teach us how to settle other, more distant worlds.

NASA Plans to Put a Base on the Moon by 2020

From the Pages of
USA TODAY

NASA plans to surpass the Apollo missions by establishing a base on the moon that could lead to a permanent human presence on the lunar surface, space agency officials said Monday.

For the first time since President Bush announced in 2004 that U.S. astronauts would return to the moon, NASA has specified what it plans to do once there. No human has set foot on the moon since 1972. That final stay, the longest, lasted three days.

Under the plans outlined Monday, human habitation of the moon would begin in 2020 with four-person crews that would stay for a week. Visits would lengthen until astronauts could live on the base for up to six months at a stretch. This could occur as early as 2024.

The Apollo missions of the 1960s and 1970s "were limited," said Doug Cooke, NASA's deputy chief of exploration. "We're looking at this more permanent capability that will allow longer stays and a lot of achievements."

Cooke and other officials declined to say precisely how much the program would cost or how it would be funded. Deputy NASA Administrator Shana Dale said the costs of building a moon colony would not require an increase in the NASA budget, currently $17 billion per year.

Last year, NASA Administrator Michael Griffin said that the first voyage back to the moon would cost $100 billion. That includes the price for NASA's new Orion spaceship, a pumped-up version of the Apollo capsule, and the Ares rocket to carry the Orion into space.

Skeptics, such as the Congressional Budget Office and the Government Accountability Office, have warned that NASA is unlikely to be able to mount such an ambitious effort with so little money. Already Griffin has cut NASA's funding of space science and aeronautics research to help pay for the moon program and the high costs of the space shuttle and the International Space Station.

Above: In one plan, unmanned, solar-powered robots would begin construction of a lunar base that would eventually be inhabited by humans.

A moon base would help NASA decide what's needed to send people to Mars, said David Portree, a former NASA historian. But he warned that the expense could sink the whole project.

"Running a base is going to be very expensive," Portree said. "It's going to make running a space station look cheap." The Congressional Research Service estimates that the station's construction cost will exceed $100 billion, more than five times the first estimate, made in the early '90s.

—Traci Watson

EPILOGUE

An Uncertain Future

THE SPACE RACE GREW LARGELY OUT OF POLITICAL competition between the United States and the Soviet Union. Putting the first astronaut into space gave the Soviets a feeling of accomplishment and national pride. Putting the first astronauts on the Moon gave Americans the same feelings. After that, many people thought it was only a matter of time before astronauts would be traveling to Mars.

But more than forty years have passed since the first Moon landing, and we are still waiting. Louis Friedman, head of the Planetary Society, in 2007 voiced frustration at the lack of progress. "In the 1960s, we imagined we would be sending a man to Mars by 1980. In the 1970s, we imagined we'd be doing it by the end of the century. . . . It's still a long way off, and it seems to be getting longer," said Friedman, whose group works to encourage the exploration of other worlds.

Left: This illustration shows an astronaut and a spacecraft on Mars. Will humans ever really travel to Mars? The question remains unanswered.

Like Friedman, many Americans feel that the U.S. space program has grown stagnant. Should we try to restore the public's appetite for space exploration? If so, what is the best way to do it? A crewed mission to the Moon or Mars might be the only way to really reignite the passion Americans felt during the space race. Yet many proposals to do just that have come and gone, and still no action has taken place.

Some say that an international effort to go to another world could stimulate the world economy, open new scientific frontiers, provide access to natural resources and energy, and rekindle a passion for space exploration. Others say that space exploration is too expensive and too dangerous, at least for crewed missions. Will the future of space exploration resemble the present, with human beings staying close to home while increasingly advanced robots and probes do our exploring for us?

Science fiction writers have envisioned countless futures in which human beings spread to other worlds and to the stars. These writers and many others say that space exploration and colonization will mark a new age of human history. Many believe this new era should start with putting people on the two worlds nearest Earth, the Moon and Mars. These worlds could serve as springboards for a whole new wave of human space settlement, they say.

To many Americans, crewed space travel—to the Moon, Mars, and beyond—promises more than just the tangible rewards of scientific knowledge, energy generation, or even human settlement. They see crewed spaceflight as a source of national pride, just as it was during the space race. "The United States global superiority depends upon a vital human space flight program," says U.S. congressman Pete Olson of Texas. "For the last 50 years, we have been the world leader economically, militarily, and scientifically. Our nation forged paths that were previously unimaginable through our willingness to make the investments and take the risks required to be the best. America prides itself on this ability and we have seen many great accomplishments as a result of this commitment."

Len Fisk, former NASA associate administrator for space science, agrees with Olson. He argues, "We should . . . be advocates for a more aggressive human spaceflight program, which is in fact capable of transforming our society, our economy, and our future: a human spaceflight program that is . . . the inspiration of our people."

Do these ideas ring true? Or do the massive expenses and harsh realities of human space travel make them nothing more than inspirational sound bites? Would space travel, industry, and colonization be a sound investment in our future? Or are they nothing more than exciting fantasies? What do you think? Should humans stay on Earth, or should they go to the Moon, Mars, and beyond?

TIMELINE

1939–1945 Nations around the world fight World War II. Military technology developed during the war provides the foundation for space technology.

1949 On February 24, the United States launches a two-stage rocket. It is the first human-made object to enter outer space.

1957 On October 4, the Soviet Union successfully launches *Sputnik 1*, the first artificial satellite to orbit Earth.

1958 The United States puts *Explorer 1*, its first artificial satellite, into orbit.

1961 Soviet cosmonaut Yuri Gagarin becomes the first human being in space on April 12. Alan Shepard becomes the first American in space on May 5. On May 25, U.S. president John F. Kennedy proposes that the United States send astronauts to the Moon by the end of the decade.

1962 NASA launches the *Mariner 2* probe, which flies past Venus.

1963 Valentina Tereshkova of the Soviet Union becomes the first woman in space.

1964 NASA launches *Mariner 4*, bound for Mars.

1967 A fire tears through the *Apollo 1* spacecraft during a pre-launch test, killing the three astronauts aboard.

1969 On July 20, the *Apollo 11* landing craft touches down on the Moon's surface. Neil Armstrong becomes the first human being to step foot on another world.

1970 The *Apollo 13* mission safely returns to Earth despite serious damage suffered during an explosion.

1971 The Soviet Union launches the first space station, Salyut 1.

1972 *Apollo 17* is the last U.S. mission to the Moon. NASA cancels the Apollo program.

1973 NASA launches Skylab, the first U.S. space station.

1975 *Viking 1* and *Viking 2* travel to Mars. Their orbiters take photos from space, while *Viking 1*'s lander touches down on the Red Planet's surface.

1977 *Voyager 1* and *Voyager 2* leave Earth to explore deep space and the outer planets.

1981 *Columbia*, the first U.S. space shuttle, launches for the first time.

1983 Sally Ride becomes the first American woman in space.

1986 On January 28, the space shuttle *Challenger* explodes on liftoff. Construction of the Russian space station Mir begins.

1989 President George H. W. Bush proposes a crewed Mars mission.

1992 The United States and Russia begin to cooperate on space exploration with an astronaut exchange.

1996 NASA scientists announce that they have found evidence of life on Mars, pointing to chemicals and structures found in the meteorite ALH84001.

1998 Construction of the International Space Station begins.

2000 A crew of three boards the International Space Station.

2003 On February 1, the shuttle *Columbia* is destroyed during reentry into Earth's atmosphere.

2004 U.S. president George W. Bush proposes a plan that would put U.S. astronauts back on the Moon by 2020. The U.S. Congress does not adopt the plan. NASA lands two rovers, *Spirit* and *Opportunity*, on the surface of Mars.

2007   Google announces its Lunar X Prize to encourage private development in space exploration.

2009   The Lunar Crater Observation and Sensing Satellite (LCROSS) launches a rocket into the Moon and finds evidence of water ice in a shadow crater.

2010   U.S. president Barack Obama proposes a new plan in which private industry would handle near-Earth spaceflight, while NASA would concentrate on deep space exploration. The Mars 500 experiment begins, with six men entering a 520-day simulation of a Mars mission. Scientist Stephen Hawking warns that people must spread out to other worlds or face extinction on Earth.

2011   NASA makes its last space shuttle flight with the launch of *Atlantis* in June. After that, NASA stops using space shuttles.

GLOSSARY

artificial satellite: a human-made object or vehicle that orbits Earth or another body in space

asteroids: rocky or metallic objects smaller than planets that orbit the Sun

atmosphere: a blanket of gases surrounding a body in space

atmospheric pressure: the weight of an atmosphere pressing down on a body in space; also called air pressure

carbon dioxide: a colorless, odorless gas made of carbon and oxygen

claustrophobia: the fear of tight or enclosed spaces

Earth orbit: the orbit of a body around the planet Earth

extinction: the complete dying out of a plant or animal species

gravity: a force that pulls bodies in space toward one another. The larger a body is, the more gravity it has.

greenhouse gas: an atmospheric gas that traps heat from the Sun, keeping the gas from escaping back out into space

habitat: housing for people in specific conditions, such as on a spacecraft

heat shield: panels on a spacecraft that protect the craft from heat generated during reentry into Earth's atmosphere

magnetic field: a zone of magnetism around an object or a body. Earth's magnetic field helps protect us from deadly radiation from the Sun.

microgravity: little to no gravity

natural satellite: a moon

nuclear energy: powerful energy created by changes inside the nucleus, or core, of an atom

orbit: to travel around another object in space; the path an object takes around another object in space

oxygen: a colorless, tasteless, and odorless gas. People need oxygen to breathe.

perfluorocarbons (PFCs): powerful manufactured greenhouse gases that are capable of trapping great amounts of heat

pressurize: to adjust the air pressure of a spacecraft, space suit, or other container to make it suitable for human beings

probe: an unpiloted spacecraft capable of sending back information from space

radiation: energy given off in waves or small particles. Much of the radiation from the Sun and other parts of space can be deadly to living things.

robotics: technology dealing with the design, construction, and operation of robots

rocket: a fuel-powered engine that pushes itself forward or upward

simulation: an imitation of a real situation, such as a spaceflight

solar power: energy derived from the Sun's light or heat

sublimate: to change from a solid into a gas

terraform: to change the atmospheric conditions of another world to make it more like Earth and therefore more hospitable to human life

zero gravity: having no gravity

SOURCE NOTES

6   Eric M. Jones, "The First Lunar Landing," NASA, March 3, 2010, http://
history.nasa.gov/alsj/a11/a11.landing.html (January 17, 2011).

7   Eric M. Jones, "One Small Step," NASA, February 16, 2010, http://history
.nasa.gov/alsj/a11/a11.step.html (January 17, 2011).

10   CNN, "Bush Unveils Mission for Moon and Beyond," CNN.com, January 15,
2004, http://www.cnn.com/2004/TECH/space/01/14/bush.space/index
.html (January 17, 2011).

10   Alan Boyle, "Stephen Hawking: Off Earth by 2110?" msnbc.com, August
9, 2010, http://cosmiclog.msnbc.msn.com/_news/2010/08/09/4850998-
stephen-hawking-off-earth-by-2110 (January 17, 2011).

11   Traci Watson, "What's Our Next Step?" *USA TODAY*, July 17, 2009.

21   Yuri Gagarin, ed., *Soviet Man in Space* (Honolulu: University Press of the
Pacific, 2001), 15–16.

22–23   John F. Kennedy, "Special Message to the Congress on Urgent National
Needs," John F. Kennedy Presidential Library and Museum, May 25,
1961, http://www.jfklibrary.org/Historical+Resources/Archives/
Reference+Desk/Speeches/JFK/Urgent+National+Needs+Page+4.htm
(January 17, 2011).

23   Harrison H. Schmitt, *Return to the Moon: Exploration, Enterprise, and
Energy in the Human Settlement of Space* (New York: Praxis Publishing,
2006), 12.

25   James A. Lovell, "Apollo Expeditions to the Moon," NASA, July 28, 1975,
http://history.nasa.gov/SP-350/ch-13-1.html (January 31, 2011).

32   Alex Steffen, "Limits and Brilliance," WorldChanging, June 19, 2007,
http://www.worldchanging.com/archives//006915.html (January 17,
2010).

37–38   CNN, "Bush Unveils Mission for Moon and Beyond."

38   Dennis Wingo, *Moonrush: Improving Life on Earth with the Moon's
Resources* (Burlington, ON: Apogee Books, 2004), 96.

39–40   Steven Siceloff, "President Outlines Exploration Goals, Promise," NASA,
April 15, 2010, http://www.nasa.gov/about/obamaspeechfeature.html
(January 17, 2011).

46   Charles Arthur, "Space Travel 'A Waste of Money,'" *Independent* (London),
April 7, 1999, http://www.independent.co.uk/news/space-travel-a-waste
-of-money-1085627.html (January 17, 2011).

51 James C. McLane, "'Spirit of the Lone Eagle': An Audacious Program for a Manned Mars Landing," *Space Review*, July 31, 2006, http://www .thespacereview.com/article/669/1 (January 17, 2011).

52–53 CNN, "Bush Space Plan Faces Opposition," CNN.com, January 14, 2004, http://www.cnn.com/2004/TECH/space/01/14/bush.opposition/index .html (January 17, 2011).

53 CNN, "Bush Unveils Mission for Moon and Beyond."

60 Dan Vergano, "Has the USA Hit Its Final Frontier in Space?" *USA TODAY*, January 19, 2010.

64 Mark Memmott, "Astronauts Face High Degree of Danger; Public Unlikely to Understand Fully, Some Experts Say," *USA TODAY*, February 3, 2003.

69 Luke Harding, "Mars Mission in a Moscow Hanger Is No Joke, Say Astronauts," *Guardian* (London), June 3, 2010, http://www.guardian .co.uk/science/2010/jun/03/mock-mission-mars-moscow-hangar (January 17, 2011).

70 Joan Arehart-Treichel, "NASA Addresses Mental Health of Mars-Mission Members," *Psychiatry News*, February 1, 2002, http://pn.psychiatryonline .org/content/37/3/5.1.full (January 17, 2011).

70 Joan Arehart-Treichel, "Psychiatrist Gains Otherworldly View of Mental Health," *Psychiatric News*, October 16, 2009, http://pn.psychiatryonline .org/content/44/20/9.1.full#sec-5 (January 17, 2011).

71 Ibid.

72 Kelly Young, "NASA Reviews Its Astronaut Screening Process," *New Scientist*, February 7, 2007, http://www.newscientist.com/article/ dn11133-nasa-reviews-its-astronaut-screening-process.html (January 17, 2011).

80 Charles Stross, "The High Frontier, Redux," *Charlie's Diary*, June 16, 2007, http://www.antipope.org/charlie/blog-static/2007/06/the_high_frontier _redux.html (January 17, 2011).

84 Douglas Wright, "Beyond the Moon: A Chat with Buzz Aldrin," *Popular Science*, July 20, 2009, http://www.popsci.com/military-aviation-amp -space/article/2009-07/beyond-moon-popsci-chats-buzz-aldrin (January 17, 2010).

85 Alex Moore, "Ethics of Terraforming," *Red Colony*, July 29, 2001, http:// www.redcolony.com/art.php?id=0107290 (January 17, 2011).

87 Boyle, "Stephen Hawking: Off Earth by 2110?"

91 Traci Watson, "Lost in Space," USA Today, September 26, 2007.

92–93 Jeff Foust, "The Future of Science and Human Spaceflight," *Space Review*, January 18, 2010, http://www.thespacereview.com/article/1547/1 (February 1, 2011).

93 Ibid.

SELECTED BIBLIOGRAPHY

National Aeronautics and Space Administration, NASA, 2011, http://www
.nasa.gov (January 18, 2011).

Raeburn, Paul. *Uncovering the Secrets of the Red Planet.* Washington, DC:
National Geographic Society, 1998.

Ridpath, Ian, and Wil Tirion. *Stars and Planets.* Princeton, NJ: Princeton
University Press, 2007.

Schmitt, Harrison H. *Return to the Moon: Exploration, Enterprise, and
Energy in the Human Settlement of Space.* New York: Praxis Publishing,
2006.

Sheehan, William, and Stephen James O'Meara. *Mars: The Lure of the Red
Planet.* New York: Prometheus Books, 2001.

Squyres, Steve. *Roving Mars: Spirit, Opportunity, and the Exploration of the
Red Planet.* New York: Hyperion, 2005.

Wingo, Dennis. *Moonrush: Improving Life on Earth with the Moon's
Resources.* Burlington, ON: Apogee Books, 2004.

Zubrin, Robert. *The Case for Mars: The Plan to Settle the Red Planet and Why
We Must.* New York: Touchstone, 1996.

ORGANIZATIONS TO CONTACT

European Space Agency (ESA)
    8-10 rue Mario Nikis
    75738 Paris Cedex 15
    France
    +33-1-5369-7654
    http://www.esa.int (This links to the ESA's English-language page.)
    The ESA is the collective space agency of eighteen European countries.
    Its goals are to establish a European presence in space, with tasks
    ranging from satellite placement to future crewed missions to other
    worlds.

NASA (National Aeronautics and Space Administration)
    NASA Headquarters
    Suite 5K39
    Washington, DC 20546-0001
    202-358-0001
    http://www.nasa.gov
    NASA is the U.S. government agency in charge of space exploration.
    NASA's scientists, engineers, and astronauts have led the way to the
    Moon landings, the space shuttle program, and the building and
    maintenance of the International Space Station.

The Planetary Society
    85 South Grand
    Pasadena, CA 91105
    626-793-5100
    http://www.planetary.org
    The Planetary Society was founded in 1980 by scientists Carl Sagan,
    Bruce Murray, and Louis Friedman. The organization's goals are
    to inspire and support planetary exploration and the search for
    extraterrestrial life.

Russian Federal Space Agency (Roscosmos)
Schepkina St. 42
Moscow, Russia 107996
499-975-44-58
http://www.federalspace.ru/main.php?lang=en (This links to the
Russian Federal Space Agency's English-language page.)
The Federal Space Agency is Russia's space exploration agency. It is
charged with space exploration and scientific development, including
the operation of Russia's *Soyuz* spacecraft.

Smithsonian National Air and Space Museum
Independence Ave at Sixth Street SW
Washington, DC 20560
202-633-2214
http://www.nasm.si.edu
The National Air and Space Museum has the world's largest collection
of historic aircraft and spacecraft. Visitors can see the *Apollo 11*
command module and touch a Moon rock.

FURTHER INFORMATION

BOOKS

Angelo, Joseph A. *Human Spaceflight*. New York: Facts on File, 2007.
Learn about the past, present, and future of crewed spaceflight,
including possible missions to and colonies on Mars.

Benge, Janet. *Alan Shepard: Higher and Faster*. Lynnwood, WA: Emerald
Books, 2007.
Read about the life and adventures of Alan Shepard, the first U.S.
astronaut in space.

Bortz, Fred. *Seven Wonders of Space Technology*. Minneapolis: Twenty-First
Century Books, 2011.
This book explores seven wonders of space technology. Learn about
the people and the science behind these amazing satellites, vehicles,
and other eqipment used to explore the farthest reaches of the solar
system.

Byers, Ann. *Neil Armstrong: The First Man on the Moon*. New York: Rosen,
2004.
Byers tells the story of Neil Armstrong, from his career as a pilot to his
time as an astronaut and his famous first steps on the Moon.

Kuhn, Betsy. *The Race for Space: The United States and the Soviet Union
Compete for the New Frontier*. Minneapolis: Twenty-First Century
Books, 2007.
Part of the award-winning People's History series, this title examines
the Cold War contest for superiority in space.

Lusted, Marcia Amidon. *The International Space Station*. Farmington Hills,
MI: Lucent, 2006.
Lusted investigates the history of space stations and the International
Space Station. She explains how the ISS was constructed, what
purposes it serves, and how it may help in future deep space
exploration.

Miller, Ron. *Mars*. Minneapolis: Twenty-First Century Books, 2006.
Miller chronicles the discovery and explorations of the planet Mars and
discusses each of its moons, its place in the solar system, and more.

——.*Robot Explorers*. Minneapolis: Twenty-First Century Books, 2008.
Learn about the unmanned missions throughout the solar system, from the first lunar and planetary probes to the sophisticated Mars rover missions.

——.*Rockets*. Minneapolis: Twenty-First Century Books, 2008.
Miller tells about the development of the rocket and its use in modern-day space travel and by the military.

——.*Space Exploration*. Minneapolis: Twenty-First Century Books, 2008.
Learn about the history of space exploration, from the earliest efforts to the shuttle program and beyond.

Robinson, Kim Stanley. *Red Mars*. New York: Spectra, 1993.
Robinson's first novel in the Red Mars trilogy begins a sweeping story of a human colonization of Mars. In this book, as well as in *Green Mars* (1994) and *Blue Mars* (1996), Robinson chronicles the colonists' competition for scarce resources, struggles for survival, and conflicts over terraforming.

Scott, Elaine. *Mars and the Search for Life*. New York: Clarion Books, 2008.
The author describes the conditions life-forms would need to survive on Mars and details efforts to search for life on the Red Planet.

Sherman, Josepha. *The Cold War*. Minneapolis: Twenty-First Century Books, 2004.
Sherman describes the political and social climate that led to the Cold War, including the space race, between the United States and the Soviet Union.

Ward, D. J. *Exploring Mars*. Minneapolis: Lerner Publications Company, 2007.
Ward takes a close look at Mars, the conditions there, the possibility of life on Mars, and the possibilities for exploring and settling the planet.

Woods, Mary B., and Michael Woods. *Space Disasters*. Minneapolis: Twenty-First Century Books, 2008.
In fifty years of space travel, more than twenty astronauts and one hundred space workers have lost their lives. With dramatic images and eyewitness accounts, this book gives a close-up look at tragic space disasters.

World Book. *Earth and Earth's Moon*. Chicago: World Book, 2007.
Learn all about the Earth-Moon system. This book includes information on the history of lunar exploration, including the Apollo missions.

——. *Mars*. Chicago: World Book, 2010.
Read about the features and exploration of Mars. This book has charts and diagrams to help readers understand Mars and the difficulties in exploring it.

WEBSITES

Astronomy Today
http://www.astronomytoday.com
Astronomy Today offers all the latest news on space, with one section devoted just to space exploration.

European Space Agency
http://www.esa.int
The ESA is the combined space agency for much of Europe. The ESA's English-language Web page includes a wealth of articles about space, space missions, and the scientific work taking place at the International Space Station.

Mars Exploration Rover Mission
http://marsrover.nasa.gov/home
This website is devoted to the Mars Rover program. Learn all about the Mars rovers, and see photographs of the Martian surface.

NASA
http://www.nasa.gov
NASA's website is loaded with information on space and space exploration. Visitors can check out photographs, articles on the latest missions and equipment, and plans for future missions.

Red Colony
http://www.redcolony.com
Red Colony is a place for people to seriously study and discuss the future exploration and colonization of Mars. The website includes a wealth of information on Mars and what it would take to put a human colony there.

Science Daily
> http://www.sciencedaily.com
> This website includes a section devoted to news and features on space science and exploration.

Space Travel
> http://www.space-travel.com
> This website tracks all the latest news in space travel, from automated and crewed flights to updates on the International Space Station and space tourism.

MOVIES

Black Sky: Winning the X Prize. DVD. Silver Spring, MD: Discovery Channel, 2004.
> Learn how Burt Rutan and his aerospace firm Scaled Composites created *SpaceShipOne*, the first private vehicle to fly into space.

Red Planet. DVD. Burbank, CA: Warner Home Video, 2001.
> Val Kilmer, Carrie-Ann Moss, Benjamin Bratt, and Simon Baker star in this sci-fi Hollywood film. The year is 2050 and humans have begun to terraform Mars.

Sci-Trek: Mining the Moon. DVD. Silver Spring, MD: Discovery Channel, 2009.
> If humans ever travel back to the Moon, they might do so to mine precious resources, such as hydrogen trapped in the lunar soil. This film from the Discovery Channel explores the possibilities.

The Universe: Colonizing Space. DVD. New York: A&E Home Video, 2010.
> This film from the History Channel uses cutting-edge, computer-generated imagery to show how humans could someday live in space.

INDEX

PHOTO ACKNOWLEDGMENTS

The images in this book are used with the permission of: © NASA/Time & Life Pictures/Getty Images, pp. 4–5; © SuperStock, p. 6; © John Chumack/Photo Researchers, Inc., pp. 8–9; NASA/GRC, p. 12; © Detlev van Ravenswaay/Glow Images, p. 16; NASA, ESA and D. Jewitt (UCLA), p. 17; © Mark Thiessen/National Geographic/ Getty Images, pp. 18–19; © Ria Novosti/Photo Researchers, Inc., pp. 21, 22; NASA/JPL, pp. 24, 33; © Science Faction/SuperStock, p. 25; © SPL/Photo Researchers, Inc., p. 26; © The Print Collector/Alamy, p. 28; © H. Darr Beiser/USA TODAY, p. 29; NASA, pp. 30, 62, 63, 71, 73, 74; © Science Source/Photo Researchers, Inc., p. 31; © Gene Blevins/LA Daily News/CORBIS, p. 34; © Mark Wilson/Getty Images, pp. 36–37; © Robert Laberge/Staff/Getty Images, p. 43; © Stocktrek Images/Getty Images, p. 52; © Bettmann/CORBIS, pp. 54–55; © Dave Welcher/Hulton Archive/Getty Images, p. 57; AP Photo/J. Scott Applewhite, p. 59; © Valerie Kuypers/AFP/Getty Images, pp. 66–67; © NASA/ZUMA Press, p. 76; © Richard Bizley/Photo Researchers, Inc., pp. 78–79, 81; © C. Butler/Photo Researchers, Inc., p. 86; © Ron Miller, p. 89; © Detlev Van Ravenswaay/Photo Researchers, Inc., pp. 90–91.

Front Cover: © Stocktrek/Photodisc/Getty Images.

Main body text set in USA TODAY Roman Regular 10.5/15.

ABOUT THE AUTHOR

Matt Doeden is a freelance author and editor living in Minnesota. He has written and edited hundreds of children's books on topics ranging from genetic engineering to rock climbing to monster trucks.